1976

SHAKESPEARE PROBLEMS

By A. W. POLLARD & J. DOVER WILSON

III
SHAKESPEARE'S HENRY VI
AND RICHARD III

SHAKESPEARE'S HENRY VI
AND RICHARD III

BY

PETER ALEXANDER

WITH AN INTRODUCTION
BY
ALFRED W. POLLARD

OCTAGON BOOKS

A DIVISION OF FARRAR, STRAUS AND GIROUX

New York   1973

First published 1929

Reprinted 1973
by permission of Cambridge University Press

OCTAGON BOOKS
A Division of Farrar, Straus & Giroux, Inc.
19 Union Square West
New York, N. Y. 10003

Library of Congress Cataloging in Publication Data

Alexander, Peter, 1893—
    Shakespeare's Henry VI and Richard III.

    Reprint of the 1929 ed., which was issued as no. 3 of
    Shakespeare problems.

    1. Shakespeare, William, 1564-1616. King Henry VI.
    2. Shakespeare, William, 1564-1616. King Richard III.
    3. Shakespeare, William, 1564-1616—Criticism, Textual.
    4. Shakespeare, William, 1564-1616—Authorship.
    I. Title.   II. Series: Shakespeare problems, 3.

PR2813.A85   1973   822.3'3   73-732
ISBN 0-374-90130-9

Printed in U.S.A. by
NOBLE OFFSET PRINTERS, INC.
New York, N.Y. 10003

PREFACE

IT was at the suggestion of the late Dr Smart that I first examined the text of *Henry VI*; and the notes which the editor of *The Times Literary Supplement* was good enough to find space for in 1924 were shaped under his criticism and that of Professor Macneile Dixon. The work on the Bad Shakespeare Quartos by Professor Pollard and Professor Dover Wilson, and Dr Greg's analysis of the Quartos of *Alcazar* and *Orlando*, were of course constantly before me. Though I have written my share in this volume since Dr Smart's death, I am still indebted to him at every turn, as those who have read his work on Shakespeare can see, and as my references, I trust, make plain.

The opportunity for a more extended examination of *Henry VI*, and its sequel *Richard III*, has been given me by the generous invitation of the editors of this series to contribute to their studies; and I have been fortunate in having Professor Pollard's help from the beginning of the new undertaking. But for his criticism my part would be even more imperfect than it is. Like other students of Shakespeare, I owe to Professor Pollard the sense of a new style and new spirit in textual criticism; and had he not provided in the first volume of the series the fixed point on which the argument rests, I should not have ventured on an attempt to remove from Shakespeare studies what seems to me a world of misapprehension.

In such a task it is impossible to eliminate friction, and difficult, with the weight of opinion against me, to be unlaborious. By trying, however, to avoid unnecessary controversy, I have done something, I hope, to escape the charge, which the acrimony of commentators provoked from Dr Johnson, that the truth to be investigated is so near to inexistence as to escape attention: for the rest, I must look to the reader's indulgence or enthusiasm for these studies.

PETER ALEXANDER

CONTENTS

CONTENTS

INTRODUCTION

By Alfred W. Pollard

I. MORE BAD QUARTOS

THE writer of this book, Mr Peter Alexander, had the good fortune in his University days to come under the influence of an inspiring teacher, Dr John Smart, whose conservative instincts in literature made him as sceptical as to the truth of many statements about Shakespeare as if he had been a born revolutionary. At the time of his premature death Dr Smart had written some chapters of an introduction to the study of Shakespeare, the publication of which,[1] incomplete as they are, by the piety of Dr Macneile Dixon and Mr Alexander, seems to me a new landmark in Shakespeare scholarship. Mr Alexander, who succeeded Dr Smart in his lectureship at Glasgow, has not only helped to preserve his teacher's work, he has been continuing it, as Dr Smart on his death-bed bade him, and has amply justified his selection for the task. His papers in *The Times Literary Supplement* (9 October and 13 November 1924) on "2 *Henry VI* and the copy for *The Contention*" and "3 *Henry VI* and *Richard Duke of York*", showing that the quartos of 1594 and 1595 are memorial reconstructions of texts which must at least have closely approximated to those which we know as 2 and 3 *Henry VI*, started a corre-

[1] *Shakespeare; Truth and Tradition*, by John Semple Smart, with a memoir by W. Macneile Dixon (Edward Arnold and Co., 1928).

spondence between us on 1–3 *Henry VI* and *Richard III*, with a view to a joint study of them as one of the "Shakespeare Problems" with which Professor Dover Wilson and I have committed ourselves to deal in this series. In the end the book has been written by Mr Alexander alone, under a fire of criticism from myself, and my task is reduced to writing this introduction.

I have a fellow-feeling with Mr Alexander because, just as nearly twenty years ago I protested (with unexpected success) against the continued acceptance of Malone's condemnation of all the early Shakespeare Quartos as "stolne and surreptitious" despite his clear recognition that in many cases they preserved good texts, from which the Folio of 1623 was in fact printed, so Mr Alexander's book is a protest against the continued acceptance of Malone's assertion (maintained despite his acknowledgment that it was formulated under a misunderstanding of Greene's attack in his *Groatsworth of Wit*) that Shakespeare began his career as a dramatist, not by writing original plays but by revising into the plays we now know as 2 and 3 *Henry VI* the versions published as *The First Part of the Contention* (1594) and *The True Tragedy of Richard Duke of York* (1595), attributed by Malone to Marlowe, Greene and Peele.

At the time Malone wrote his famous dissertation, there had been no general revival of interest in the Elizabethan drama as a whole, and the inclination to present the genius of Shakespeare as a literary miracle was at its height. It thus did not occur to Malone, or to his critics, that to hand over the work of the best-known playwrights of the day to be improved by a young actor, whose lack of education (in order to enhance the literary miracle) the builders of the theory were simultaneously exaggerating, was not a course which the sharers in any Elizabethan Company of players would lightly have thought of adopting. Unfortunately the sanity Malone displayed in marshalling his arguments has impressed students much more than their too frequent lack of connection with his ultimate conclusions; thus most present-day students, while yet young and uncritical, have learnt to believe that Shakespeare did as a fact pass some years "in the workshop" with the patching of old plays as his main employment. Without denying that he may have done some such jobs we may reasonably give sympathetic consideration to the supposition that before being called to improve other men's work he had some successes to his credit as sole or part author of one or more original plays.

As I have said, one of the most important features of Mr Alexander's book is his claim that *The First part of the Contention betwixt the two famous Houses of Yorke and Lancaster*, printed by Thomas Creede for Thomas Millington in 1594 (after entry on the Stationers' Register on March 12) and *The true Tragedie of Richard Duke of Yorke as it was sundrie times acted by the Right Honourable the Earle of Pembrooke his seruants*, printed in 1595 by P. S. (Peter Short) for Thomas Millington, were just Bad Quartos of the plays we know as 2 and 3 *Henry VI*; so to Bad Quartos I must once more recur.

In the articles published in 1918 in *The Times Literary Supplement* on "The Stolne and Surreptitious Texts of Shakespeare" by Professor Dover Wilson and myself I think we made some contribution to their elucidation by contending that they could have been more easily produced by actors who had taken part in the plays than by a knavish publisher sending a shorthand writer to the theatre. We were also on the right track in thinking that the plague years, 1592–3, were a likely time at which such texts might have originated. But besides burdening our theory by taking over Fleay's supposition that when actors were about to start on a provincial tour the London texts would have been specially abridged for their use—a disputable proposition which Mr W. J. Lawrence promptly disputed, though I think the weight of opinion is against him—we were still so far hypnotized by the old idea of the wicked publisher that we took it for granted that it was for the sake of the money which could be obtained from a publisher that the bad texts were put together. I believe that for such texts the money would have been so small as to make their construction hardly worth while and that with such an origin some at least of the publishers concerned would have refused to touch them.

A new advance was made by Dr Greg, who first in an article on "Bad Quartos outside Shakespeare", contributed as "a preliminary investigation" to *The Library* in October 1919 and subsequently in 1923 in his *Two Elizabethan Stage Abridgements*: The Battle of Alcazar *and* Orlando Furioso, *an essay in critical bibliography,* published by the Clarendon Press and very kindly dedicated to the authors of the articles in *The Times Literary Supplement,* produced positive grounds for belief both that legitimate abridged texts were in use and, on the other hand, that texts made up by actors mainly from memory, but with occasional help from their "parts", almost certainly originated with actors stranded in the provinces and obliged to make up, as best they could, something popular to play. As Mr Alexander sets forth in his text, supplementary evidence came through the revival by Mr Crompton Rhodes[1] of the parallel case, originally adduced (though not followed up) by George Steevens, of the similar reconstruction of Sheridan's *School for Scandal* in the provinces and the publication of this stolen text in advance of the true one. That reconstruction from memory and actors' parts is at least an element in the origin of the Bad Quartos of Shakespeare, *Romeo and Juliet* (1597), *Henry V*, the *Merry Wives*, and *Hamlet* (1603) is now, if not generally, at least very widely accepted, and those who wish to believe in the honesty of publishers can plead that there is a considerable difference between sending a shorthand writer to a London theatre to take down what he could of the words spoken by the players, and buying a ready-made text from the men who had been playing it in the provinces.

As soon as Dr Greg had suggested that the Bad Quartos had been brought into existence by methods which were not confined to four plays, it became probable that the class would be further extended, and by his articles in *The Times Literary Supplement*, Mr Alexander (in another "preliminary investigation" here more fully worked out) made a good case for *The First Part of the Contention* and *The True Tragedy of Richard Duke of York* having originated in the same way. His theory as stated in *The Times*

---

[1] In two articles in *The Times Literary Supplement* in September 1925. See also Mr Rhodes' paper, "Some Aspects of Sheridan Bibliography", read before the Bibliographical Society, 15 October 1928, and printed in *The Library*, 4th Series, IX, 233–61.

Literary Supplement is already winning acceptance, and I think that his subsequent application of it to *The Taming of a Shrew*, though it rests on a much narrower basis, has no intrinsic improbability as soon as it is realized that a member of a company of stranded actors may very well have been not only a vamper, but a fluent one, who did not worry about piecing together fragments of passages for which it was easy for him to improvise substitutes.

For our present purpose *The Taming of a Shrew*, though it raises some of the same problems, may be put on one side. But *The First Part of the Contention* and *The True Tragedy of Richard Duke of York* are crucial. If these, as Mr Alexander maintains, are simply memorial reconstructions of texts closely similar to those which have come down to us as 2 and 3 *Henry VI*, then not only Malone's arguments, but all subsequent deductions from their discrepancies, their borrowings from this or that author and their verbal resemblances to the work of Peele, Greene and Marlowe count for nothing, just as Malone's argument that in his *Groatsworth of Wit* Greene in his phrase "beautified with our feathers" was accusing Shakespeare of plagiarism now counts (or should count) for nothing, because it is clearly a misinterpretation.[1] All these arguments (from the texts of the *Contention* and *True Tragedy* where they differ from 2 and 3 *Henry VI*) are indeed the more absolutely dead of the two, because from Greene's invective we remain entitled to ask how he came to be so angry with Shakespeare in August 1592, whereas as regards parallels and reminiscences and quotations from other plays which had recently been acted there is no reason

[1] See pages 44–49.

to ask how these got into memorial reconstructions. From the very nature of the case a vamped text would be likely to contain phrases and even lines from other plays in which its authors had lately been acting and we know that they got into the Bad Quarto of *Hamlet* and other piracies.

Thus, as regards authorship, if Mr Alexander is right, we must turn down the Quartos of 1594 and 1595 altogether and argue from the text of 2 and 3 *Henry VI* as it stands in the Folio and from nothing else, and with no prepossession whatever in favour of the theory that Shakespeare was in the habit of re-handling other men's plays. We must in fact start afresh.

II. SHAKESPEARE'S EARLIEST WORK

Just as Malone misapplied the phrase "stolne and surreptitious" despite his knowledge of the quality of the Good Quartos, and continued to maintain that Shakespeare had rehandled the work of Marlowe, Greene and Peele after abandoning his contention that Greene's attack in the *Groatsworth* involved a charge of plagiarism, so (as Mr Alexander notes) in dealing with the traditions as to Shakespeare's youth he threw over his own admirable exposition as to how such traditions should be tested. I agree with Dr Smart and Mr Alexander that, judged by Malone's principles, the best authenticated tradition is that reported by Aubrey (a humble follower of Herodotus in his readiness to put down all he heard) on the authority of the younger Beeston, whose father had been in Shakespeare's company, that before he came to London Shakespeare had been a schoolmaster. With a little more subtlety Malone might have

accepted this as enhancing the miracle that neverthe-
less he wrote his plays. But Malone was under the
influence of Farmer, who, not content with destroying
the theory of Shakespeare's "learning", denied him
such moderate proficiency in Latin as other Stratford
boys are known to have attained. If we can clear all
the merely sensational gossip out of our heads so far
as to permit ourselves to believe that the Stratford
Grammar School was ordinarily efficient and that
Shakespeare went to it, and in his teens was not ex-
traordinarily dull, the "small Latin" with which Ben
Jonson credits him should have included at least a
little Virgil, a little Ovid, a little Plautus and a little
Seneca, besides some study of such school books as
the *Apothegmata* of Erasmus as translated by Udall,
from which an illusive appearance of wide reading
was easily won. Most of the playwrights of the
'eighties were University men, and it seems in accordance with human nature that a Stratford
Grammar School man should think it necessary in
competition with them to stretch his Latin as far as
it would go rather than pose as the possessor of
"native woodnotes wild", even as, when he turned to
narrative poetry, he wrote on Venus and Adonis and
on Lucrece rather than on English themes. On this
view the plays which show the most classical influence,
*Titus Andronicus, The Comedy of Errors, The Taming
of the Shrew*, would be the real products of his workshop days, and despite verse tests or any other evidence
of the kind I should like to see them assigned to the
earliest possible dates. The dates can only be got back
as early as I should like by supposing that the "old
plays" which Professor Dover Wilson is driven by his
analysis to believe that Shakespeare had before him

when writing the two comedies, were his own early efforts or plays in which he had at least had a hand, and that *Titus and Vespasian* (Henslowe's *Tittus ana Vespasia*), which on the evidence of the contemporary German version of *Titus Andronicus* Sir Edmund Chambers regards as a possible earlier version of it, was also, in whole or in part, from his own pen. Much against my will I have been converted to the opinion that the combined evidence of the inclusion of *Titus Andronicus* in the Folio of 1623 and its mention as Shakespeare's by Francis Meres in 1598 is not adequately met by admitting—fastidiously—that Shakespeare may have touched up the play here and there, or added a few lines of his own. Thus in the absence of any evidence to the contrary, other than the literary connoisseurship which I very largely distrust, I feel bound to work on the basis that the *Titus Andronicus*, which was produced at the Rose under Henslowe's auspices (with his note *ne*, interpreted as *new* or newly revised) by the Earl of Sussex's men on 24 January 1594, was in whole or part by Shakespeare. I think, moreover, that the play called by Henslowe *Tittus and Vespasia* produced (also at the Rose and also marked by Henslowe *ne*) on 15 April 1592 by the company whose patron, afterwards for a few months Earl of Derby, was then known as Lord Strange, in the absence of any evidence to the contrary should also, if it is to be accepted as an earlier version of *Andronicus*, be considered as in whole or part written by Shakespeare. From 15 April to 23 June 1592 it was performed altogether seven times, and though other plays were acted more often it had the highest average receipts of the season, Henslowe's share for each performance working out

at the rate of £2. 8s. 6d., with £2. 3s. 6d. for Marlowe's *Jew of Malta* as the next best.¹ Thus there

¹ I am the more inclined to believe that despite the unhappi-
ness of the title which Henslowe bestowed on the earlier of them,
the two *Titus* plays are thus connected because on the title page
of the (long lost) 1594 edition of *Titus Andronicus* printed and
published by John Danter and duly entered on the Stationers'
Register on 6 February 1594, i.e. during the few months in
which the former Lord Strange bore the title of Earl of Derby,
the play is said to have been "plaide by the Right Honourable
the Earle of Darbie, Earle of Pembrooke and Earle of Sussex
their seruants", and I feel bound to assume that the order in
which the companies are named on this contemporary title
page is correct. Before the entry of this edition we have no
knowledge of Pembroke's men as playing except between
October 1592 and some date in August 1593, i.e. five or six
weeks before 28 September 1593 when Henslowe wrote to
Alleyn that they had been back in town for some such time,
destitute. They may have sold one copy of the play to Danter
and another to Henslowe, or direct to Sussex's men who performed it under Henslowe's auspices on 24 January 1594. But
if it was the earliest of the three mentioned on the title the
performance by the Earl of Derby's men must have preceded
this date and be referred to the time before Lord Strange
succeeded to the Earldom. If so, to those who know Henslowe's
carelessness as to titles it is unnecessary to assume that the
company was at the same time possessed of one play called *Titus
Andronicus* and another which he called *Tittus and Vespasia*.

Since opinions to this effect were expressed in this introduction as first written I have had the pleasure of reading a paper
on "Shakespeare and *Titus Andronicus*" by Mr Austin K.
Gray (*Studies in Philology*, published by the University of
Carolina Press, xxv, 295–311). In this he shows that Meres
was "in a favourable position" for knowing the authorship of
Titus through his intimacy with Nashe, who (besides having
books printed by its printer, John Danter, in 1592–3–4) was
living in Danter's house. Mr Gray also adduces a striking
series of parallels between *Titus* and both *Venus and Adonis*
and *Lucrece*, and argues from them that the version of *Titus*
performed as "new" on 23 January 1594, half-way between
the entry of these two poems on the Stationers' Register

could have been no financial discontent with the play
which might have caused someone who had no hand
in it to be asked to act as its reviser, even if revision of
a living playwright's work by another hand for such
reasons were a better established practice than seems
to be the case.

   Titus and Vespasian is important for our purpose
because on 3 March 1592, six weeks before its
production, Lord Strange's players had produced,
with Henslowe's note of *ne* in his record, the play of
Harey the vj, as he called it, and this has generally
been identified with the 1 *Henry VI* of the Folio of
1623 on the ground of the presence in this last of the
Talbot scenes (iv, ii–vii) which seem precisely fitted
to have provoked the outburst in Nashe's *Pierce
Penilesse* (licensed 8 August 1592).

   How would it have ioyed braue *Talbot* (the terror of the
French) to thinke that after he had lyne two hundred
yeares in his Tombe, hee should triumphe againe on the
Stage, and haue his bones newe embalmed with the teares
of ten thousand spectators at least (at seuerall times), who
in the Tragedian that represents his person, imagine they
behold him fresh bleeding. (McKerrow's *Nashe*, i, 212.)

I agree in this identification and thus find myself

(18 April 1593 and 9 May 1594) was (though only to a very
slight extent in the first Act) a revision by Shakespeare of an
earlier play on the subject. That such an earlier play existed
Mr Gray is content to deduce from the allusion to the opening
scene of *Titus* in *A Knack to Know a Knave*, entered on the
Stationers' Register, 7 January 1594, without discussing, or
indeed mentioning, Sir Edmund Chambers' identification of it
with the *Titus and Vespasian* acted on 15 April 1592. Since
A Knack was marked as *ne* by Henslowe less than two months
later (10 June 1592) this allusion favours Sir Edmund's identification and has been quoted by him.

temporarily at variance with Mr Alexander who prefers to believe that Shakespeare at this time had no connection with Strange's men, but probably had been connected for two or three years with Lord Pembroke's. The main objection to sharing this belief is that, as Sir Edmund Chambers has pointed out, we have no certain knowledge, and indeed only the scantiest reason to believe, that a Pembroke company existed before 1592, and while Mr Alexander has a right to claim that the play-loving lord of two years or so before 1593 mentioned in Kyd's letter to Puckering (*The Works of Thomas Kyd*, edited by F. S. Boas, 1901, p. lxiv) as objecting to Marlowe's atheism may have been the Earl of Pembroke, Sir Edmund Chambers has preferred to identify him with Lord Strange and Dr Boas to identify him with Lord Fitzwalter, who became fifth Earl of Sussex on 14 December 1593. Under these circumstances it again seems to me uneconomical to suppose that Strange's men were acting a Henry VI play in which Shakespeare had no hand, while a possibly non-existent company of Lord Pembroke's were acting that printed as Shakespeare's in the Folio of 1623, and this in face of the probability that an earlier version of *Titus Andronicus* was being played by Strange's men simultaneously with their *Harey the vj*. Mr Alexander's belief that Shakespeare had belonged about 1590 to Pembroke's men is, however, widely shared at the present day, and there may be an advantage in his arguing his case on these premises, which, though I think them precarious, cannot be summarily rejected as impossible. Moreover, while I think that the balance of evidence points to Shakespeare having written for Strange's men early in 1592, I agree that there is no positive evidence that he was acting for them then, and nothing that compels belief that he had either written or acted for them before that year, though there appears to be room for a supposition that he had done so.

The strength of the case for Shakespeare's connection either with Strange's men or Pembroke's before 1592 being so slight I am tempted to draw attention to another possibility, viz. that Shakespeare gained his first experience as an actor by playing, not with Strange's men or with Pembroke's (which I agree with Sir Edmund Chambers in regarding as an offshoot of Strange's formed for travelling in the late spring of 1592) but with the Queen's. It is improbable that the suggestion has not been made already (I am far from having read all that has been written on the subject) and there may be good grounds for rejecting it. But it seems worth while to see what can be said in its support.

III. SHAKESPEARE A QUEEN'S MAN

My first impulse to investigate the possibility that Shakespeare began his theatrical career by acting with the Queen's men (possibly joining them when they visited Stratford in 1586 or 1587) came from my desire to find an answer to the question which, it seems to me, we are bound to ask, "why was Greene in August 1592, when he wrote his *Groatsworth of Wit*, so angry with Shakespeare?" So long as the phrase "an upstart Crow, beautified with our feathers" was interpreted as conveying a charge that Shakespeare had used as his own the work of the men whom Greene was addressing and of Greene himself, the answer was easy. If Marlowe, Peele and Greene had,

as Malone supposed, written the Henry VI plays in
an earlier form between them, and Shakespeare had
rewritten or in any way rehandled them, then Greene
would have had a real cause for being angry himself
and for inciting the others to anger, even though,
according to the accepted interpretation of such
evidence as we possess, playwrights were in the habit of
selling their work absolutely to this or that company
of players, and the players thus could claim that they
had a right to call in anyone they pleased to better
the work if he could. In 1592 playwrights did not
talk about insults to their art, but they were human
enough, with some jealousy of each other (as Greene
certainly had of Marlowe) and some special jealousy
also of any rival who could not boast that he had been
educated at Oxford or Cambridge, as Greene boasted
on his title pages that he had taken his degree at both.
The reason why Greene's attack was misinterpreted
by at least one contemporary (R. B. in his well-
known lines in *Greenes Funeralls*[1]), why Malone,
when he had clearly seen the true meaning, could not
get away from the influence of the wrong one, and
why for over a century this influence of the wrong
one has dominated Shakespeare criticism, is that the
misinterpretation (when the facts are so represented
as to fit it) makes such attractively good sense. Yet,
as Mr Alexander has shown, the phrase "beautified
with our feathers" applied to the "upstart Crow"
must be construed on the same lines as the earlier

---

[1] Greene gaue the ground to all that wrote vpon him.
    Nay more the men that so eclipst his fame
    Purloynde his Plumes, can they deny the same?
(*Greenes Funeralls*, by R. B. Gent. Printed by John Danter,
1594. Sonnet ix, ll. 12–14.)

phrases "Puppets that spake from our mouths", "Anticks garnisht in our colours" applied in general abuse of the players of the day. Greene in his vanity was claiming all the credit of a successful play for the playwright, disregarding the contribution of the player, and his wrath was aroused by no worse injury than the spectacle of one of this despised class (against which at the moment he had a grievance for not relieving his distress) daring to thrust himself into competition with the University playwrights.

It must be acknowledged that the explanation of Greene's wrath here set forth is not nearly so striking as the wrong one and although it is notorious that the true cause of violent indignation is often absurdly inadequate we must not make our true interpretation in this case more inadequate than it need be. We must not think that Greene was merely generalizing. It was "*our* colours", "*our* mouths", "*our* feathers", and since *our* means "yours and mine" and Greene was very much of an egoist, I think we may be sure that while, to keep to the letter of our document, we must expect Shakespeare to have acted in plays by the three dramatists whom Greene is addressing, he had certainly acted in plays by Greene. Now in the season at the Rose theatre, owned by Henslowe in the first half of 1592, along with *Titus and Vespasian* and *Harry VI* there had been acted by Lord Strange's men (reinforced by Edward Alleyne, the Lord Admiral's servant) Marlowe's *Jew of Malta*, *A Knack to Know a Knave*, which has been identified, rightly or wrongly, with the play to which Greene alludes when he addresses Nashe as "yong *Iuuenall*, that byting Satyrist, that lastly with mee together writ a Comedie", a play called by Henslowe *Muly Mollocco*

which may indicate Peele's *Battle of Alcazar*, also
Greene's own plays, *Orlando Furioso* and *Friar Bacon
and Friar Bungay*, and *A Looking Glass for London*
written in collaboration with Lodge. Thus it is
open to anyone, who wishes to believe that Shakespeare was acting regularly with Lord Strange's men
during this season at the Rose, to contend that this was
the time when the puppet Shakespeare had spoken
from the mouths of Greene and all the three playwrights whom he addresses, when the "antick" had
been "garnisht" in their colours and the "upstart
Crow" beautified with their feathers. It may well be
so, for as Dr Greg has pointed out to me, although
Shakespeare is not mentioned in the plot of the *Seven
Deadly Sins* acted (if the identification of the players
called by their Christian names with members of the
company be accepted) by Lord Strange's men some
time before 1592, he may have taken the part of
King Henry VI as one of the two commentators who
sat throughout the play in a gallery and did not need
to be called for their parts, and if he was acting at all
in that season, and not devoting himself exclusively
to writing plays, it would be to Lord Strange's Company that he belonged. But though Greene may
have had these plays by Marlowe, Peele and himself
in his mind, I do not think that they suffice. The
malicious misquotation "Tygers hart wrapt in a
Players hyde" shows that the play we know as
3 *Henry VI* (originally, no doubt, entitled *The True
Tragedy of Richard Duke of York*, as in the quarto of
1595) was already in existence, and it is difficult to
see when or where it could have been acted in London
in 1592. If it was earlier than 1592 and Shakespeare
wrote it, then he was already himself a playwright

before he was beautified with the feathers provided
for him by other playwrights during that particular
season, and we must not believe that the Talbot
scenes to which Nashe alludes were his first contribution to the drama. Moreover Greene's egoism and
anger seem to me to require a much longer and more
personal provision of feathers than his plays had
offered in that short season of 1592, and this as far as
we know could only have come about if Shakespeare
had been for some considerable time a member of the
Queen's company for which Greene had written all
or most of his plays.[1]

Of the three playwrights whom Greene was
addressing, Marlowe had no connection with the
Queen's company and in putting together my case
I am not very willing to rely on the possibility that
Shakespeare may have acted in 1592 as a Strange's
man in *The Jew of Malta* and so have worn some
of Marlowe's feathers. I would rather claim that
Greene was not addressing Marlowe in the same

   [1] Sir Edmund Chambers notes that *A Looking Glass for
London and England* and *The Scottish History of James the
fourth* both seem to have had a Queen's actor, John Adams, in
the original cast; *Friar Bacon and Friar Bungay* and also
Selimus, if that be Greene's, are stated on the title pages of the
published texts to have been "plaid by Her Maiesties Seruants"
and "the Queenes Maiesties Players", and *Orlando Furioso* is
the play of which the author of the *Defence of Cony-Catching*
(entered on the Stationers' Register, 21 April 1592) bade
Greene "aske the Queen's Players if he had not sold it them
for twenty Nobles, and when they were in the country, sold
the same play to the Lord Admiral's men for as much more".
The comical history of Alphonsus King of Aragon published in
1599 as "by R. G.", no doubt with the intention of the
initials being accepted as standing for Greene, as it is
by most critics, merely stated "as it hath bene sundrie times
Acted", without specifying the name of a Company.

spirit as the other two, but merely trying to get him into trouble. As to what plays Nashe had written, or where they were acted nothing seems to be known, but in his *Have with you to Saffron Walden*, while rather meanly anxious to make out that Greene had "subscribed" to him rather than he to Greene, he felt bound to add "in anything but plotting plaies, wherein he (Greene) was his craft's master". If Greene was, as thus indicated, Nashe's leader in writing plays, since, as we know, he wrote for the Queen's men, it may be claimed that there is some likelihood that Nashe wrote for them also. As to the third man, to whom Greene writes "were it not an idolatrous oth, I would sweare by sweet S. George, thou art unworthy better hap, sith thou dependest on so meane a stay", this is universally acknowledged to be George Peele, and of Peele we know from the printed edition that his *Old Wives Tale* was written for "the Queenes Maiesties players" not very long before 1592, or, as Dr Greg puts it, about 1590. Unhappily the quarto of *The Famous Chronicle of King Edward I*, also by Peele, gives no information as to the company by which it was played, and the fact that it is generally placed either immediately after or immediately before *The Old Wives Tale* as an argument for assigning it to the same company carries no great weight. Our ignorance here is the more regrettable because it is in this play, at the end of the scene in which Edward assigns the crown of Scotland to Baliol, that Queen Elinor speaks the four congratulatory lines:

Now braue John Baliol Lord of Galloway,
And King of Scots shine with thy golden head!
Shake thy spears, in honour of his name
Under whose royalty thou wearest the same.

Sir Edmund Chambers remarks that as evidence that
Shakespeare acted in this play "this is not very convincing". But the flatness of the rhyming couplet is
so glaring that I doubt whether Peele at his worst
could have written it, save for the sake of a friendly
pun on the name of the actor who (subsequently
known for his fondness for royal parts) was playing
Edward I. It is very provoking that Abel Jeffes in
the edition he published in 1593 did not trouble to
state by what company or companies the play had
been acted. But at any rate we have this evidence
of Shakespeare having acted in a play by Peele in
addition to those played in 1592.

While I cannot claim more than some probability
that *Edward I* was a Queen's play my adventure in
looking for what can be said for connecting Shakespeare with the Queen's men is certainly strengthened
by the fact that he took over all or part of the plots of
three old Queen's plays. These are *The Troublesome
Reign of King John*, in two parts, "publicly acted by
the Queens Maiestys players" imprinted for Sampson
Clarke in 1591; *The most famous chronicle historye of
Leire King of England and his three daughters*,
licensed for publication to Edward White 14 May
1594 (earliest extant edition 1605) and acted by the
Queen's men and Sussex's in the previous April at the
Rose, the presumption being that it was an old
Queen's play of which Henslowe was then in control;
and lastly, *The famous victories of Henrye the Fyft*,
licensed to Thomas Creede, also on 14 May 1594
(earliest extant edition 1598), which is associated with
the Queen's men by a story about Tarlton, and must
therefore have been acted before his death on
3 September 1588. As far as what I have called

literary connoisseurship can prove anything I think
Mr Dugdale Sykes in his *Sidelights on Shakespeare*
(pp. 99–142) made a fair case for believing that the
Troublesome Reign and *Leire* are by the same man
and that man George Peele. We have no such
evidence (except on the old theory as to the relation
of the two *Shrew* plays) of Shakespeare treating other
old plays in this way, and although all three plays
may have been in print by the end of 1594, and
John three years earlier, and therefore available for
adaptation, the fact that all three plays were written
afresh, with only a few verbal resemblances may
suggest that Shakespeare was trusting to his memory
of how they went rather than adapting from a printed
text in front of him.

It will rightly be said that as positive evidence that
Shakespeare began his career as an actor with the
Queen's men all this amounts to very little, but little
as it may be it is more than can be adduced for
connecting him with either Strange's or Pembroke's
(if it existed) before 1592, it seems to me to make
Greene's attack on him more comprehensible, and
presents no difficulty to the supporters of the two
other companies. For if the Queen's men offered,
as they must have seemed to do before the death of
Tarlton, the best opening to a man desirous of earning
his living as an actor in 1586 or 1587, by the end of
1590, and perhaps a little earlier, when Shakespeare
was commencing dramatist, it would certainly have
been a good company to quit, as its failing fortunes
caused it to act mainly in the country, which must have
offered many obstacles to writing plays. Moreover,
while there is little or no evidence of the Queen's
men commissioning new plays they were beginning

to sell old ones which other companies still found actable, and it seems likely that the young playwright would wish to work for one of these. He may or may not have joined Strange's men as an actor, but I believe that he was certainly writing for them in 1592, and on the hypothesis of Sir Edmund Chambers that Lord Pembroke's company was formed by a friendly arrangement in the spring of that year out of the overgrown company of Lord Strange, there is no reason why he should not have written for Pembroke's men also, except that they would probably have been content with a stock of well-known old plays to take into the country. Shakespeare himself would surely, after he began writing, have gone on tour as little as possible, and that he who won the Earl of Southampton's favour in April 1593 should have been one of the unhappy men who returned broken from the country the following August is quite incompatible with all we know of his business ability and the eagerness with which he pursued Southampton's friendship. If we take into consideration the chaotic theatrical conditions in 1592 the fact that Pembroke's men were in possession of some of Shakespeare's plays is no proof that Shakespeare acted for them.

IV. HAD SHAKESPEARE A COLLABORATOR?

I have explored what seems to me the possibility that Shakespeare began his career as an actor with the Queen's men not from a mischievous impulse to confuse issues already confused enough, but because, as things stand, any theory which takes for granted that Shakespeare was a member of Strange's company is apt to be summarily dismissed by those who believe that he belonged to Lord Pembroke's, while students who, like Mr Alexander, assume that he was writing for Pembroke's men before 1592 run a risk of receiving equally scant consideration. This third suggestion may at least remind even those who reject it that we simply do not know to what company Shakespeare belonged as an actor before he joined the Lord Chamberlain's men in the autumn of 1594 and that while the strain which the plague imposed on all the companies was at its height he probably did the best he could for himself with his usual business ability.

Mr Alexander's case, as presented in this volume of the *Shakespeare Problems* series, covers a wide ground, and there are many individual points in his exposition as to which, even after all our discussions, I remain doubtful, possibly because I grew up under the influence of Furnivall and Dowden and Mr Alexander under the tuition of Dr Smart. I am wholeheartedly in agreement with him in regarding *The First Part of the Contention* and *The True Tragedy* as Bad Quartos, debased forms of plays written before 1592 and substantially the same as 2 and 3 *Henry VI*, not themselves the texts out of which 2 and 3 *Henry VI* were subsequently developed, and I agree also that any parallels with Marlowe found in these Bad Quartos and not in 2 and 3 *Henry VI* must be written off. I am also wholeheartedly in agreement with Mr Alexander as to the unlikelihood of Shakespeare in his early days having been set to revise plays by such senior dramatists as Marlowe, Greene and Peele. Moreover, in the absence of any certain knowledge that any two of these three ever produced plays in collaboration, and the extreme improbability that

Marlowe and Greene could ever have written together, I think that the argument from parallels and reminiscences may fairly be inverted and that any play in which it has been suggested that all these three dramatists had a hand is intrinsically more likely to have been written by an actor familiar with plays of the trio than by all three of them in collaboration. On the other hand, I cannot regard the inclusion of all the four plays 1–3 *Henry VI* and *Richard III* in the Folio of 1623 (some thirty years after they were written) as implying any personal guarantee by Heminge and Condell that they were each and all the unaided work of Shakespeare. Even when reinforced by such deductions as may be drawn from the exclusion of *Pericles* from the Folio such a theory seems to involve an anachronism. It would not be fair to quote the sixteenth-century editions of Chaucer as in any way parallel to the seventeenth-century editions of Shakespeare, but Heminge and Condell grew up in the uncritical atmosphere in which such editions, with their mass of patently un-Chaucerian matter, were possible, and they thus seem to me not in the least likely to have seriously considered the exclusion of plays from the Folio because someone besides Shakespeare may have had a hand in them.

While claiming the liberty to admit collaboration in these plays, despite Heminge and Condell's silence as to it, if sufficient evidence can be produced, I have no desire to over-estimate the evidence which remains when old prepossessions are shaken off. Greene himself must, I think, go out, as if he had any charge of the appropriation of his own work to bring he would have brought it much more loudly. If he disappears I could wish that there should disappear a purple passage from my Shakespeare Lecture to the British Academy in 1924 but I fear I must endure the nemesis which purple passages justly provoke, and that it was not any fear of Greene's Ghost that made Shakespeare so criminally careless as to the fate of his own plays. About Nashe as far as I am aware no one has ever worried, though he remains in the same boat as Marlowe and Peele. As to Marlowe I fall back on an old formula of my own by which, until my class at King's College, London, dragged me into it, I kept out of this controversy: (i) if Shakespeare ever set himself to imitate Marlowe what he wrote would be indistinguishable from Marlowe at his best; (ii) there is no room for both Shakespeare and Marlowe in any one of the four plays. Thus despite the development of Crookback's character on two widely different lines, (1) as full of high courage and delight in the courage of others, full also of family feeling, (2) a mere bloody hypocritical villain, I cannot deny that the bright gallantry may be a sketch by Shakespeare in rivalry with Marlowe, while the self-portrayal in the less attractive character in 3 *Henry VI*, Act III, sc. ii, ll. 124–95, may have been dictated by a sudden recollection of the requirements of the plot as it was to be developed in *Richard III*. Is it justifiable to call in Marlowe when it is possible to do without him, and if we refrain from calling in Greene, Nashe or Marlowe is it reasonable to call in Peele, who is notoriously called in by every theorizer about plays of this period who wants to account for a quantity of quiet dull verse? I confess I want Peele so bitterly in 1 *Henry VI* to shoulder the Joan of Arc libels (as a pair to his libels on Queen Elinor in *Edward I*), and in *Richard III* to take the blame for the interminable flyting between Richard and his mother and wife, that I am loth to give him up. Whether this is a mere instance of the weakness of wanting Shakespeare always to be at his best, or can be seriously justified depends I think on whether these four plays do or do not show any convincing evidence of double authorship. Mr Alexander has dealt with some of the evidence which has been adduced by Fleay and others (the others including myself in my articles in *The Times Literary Supplement* on "The York and Lancaster Plays", though in his amiability he has only mentioned my name when we agree), but much seems to me still to remain, and if Shakespeare had any collaborator in these four plays I cannot help believing it was Peele.

My only doubt as to the presence of a collaborator arises from my strong inclination to believe that any great amount of interruption in writing a play might produce many discrepancies in the work of a single playwright of the same kind as those which suggest double authorship. I am sure that neither of 1 *Henry VI* nor of *Richard III* was the extant text written scene by scene in any orderly fashion, that the excessive length (3619 lines) of *Richard III* must be partly explained by recognizing as interpolations the impossible appearances and speeches of the dethroned Queen Margaret and the subsequent references to her prophecies, and that so many additions appear to have been made to 1 *Henry VI* that probably some scenes in the play as first written were taken out to make room for them. I incline to believe that 1 *Henry VI* was originally written by Shakespeare in collaboration with Peele, but I am the less anxious to press this belief against Mr Alexander's because the bibliographical evidence which has been found in other plays that Shakespeare was blending new work and old need not, I think, be taken to prove that he was recasting other men's old work rather than his own, or that this old work had necessarily been completed and put on the stage. Shakespeare must surely have made his false starts like other men and occasionally even have got some way with a play and then put it aside to work at another likely at the moment to win greater success. Since he was a thrifty man nothing would be more probable than that he should keep his papers and when he took them up again should use as much of them as he found acceptable, and occasionally blunder over his joins. Whether or no he was sole author of 1 *Henry VI* as first written, our extant text of it stands out as an example of the result of repeated and drastic rehandlings, just as *King John* stands out as an example of the construction of an entirely new play on the lines of an old one, and *A Midsummer Night's Dream* (since Professor Dover Wilson edited it) stands out as providing an instance of the lift which Shakespeare could give to an old scene by putting some new poetry into it.

V. VERSE TESTS

As regards 1 *Henry VI* I hope the Talbot battle scenes will not continue to be dated especially early in Shakespeare's career because they happen to be mostly in rhyme. That the "rhyme test", like the other verse tests, has some degree of validity must be conceded because these tests played a great part in establishing the sequence of Shakespeare's plays in an approximate order which, roughly speaking, confirms and is confirmed by such other evidence as has come to light. But that the tests have proved useful in this way does not compel us to believe that they have any intrinsic validity in themselves, or that Shakespeare deliberately abandoned one medium of expression for another because he was dissatisfied with the old ones. Such validity as can be claimed for the verse tests is due to the fact that things which vary with the same things vary, at least to some extent, with each other. The real changes were in Shakespeare's outlook on life and the themes and the method of treating them which this changing outlook, in combination with the demands of the theatre, led him to take up. His choice of mediums of expression changed with these changes. At the outset without anything very profound to say he found rhymed verse (which I think the actors raised their voices to deliver) useful to give point to his epigrams and to say pretty things prettily; a little later we find it used, e.g. in *Richard II*, in contrast with unrhymed verse to hint insincerity, and both there and in 1 *Henry VI*, when, as a Victorian critic may be allowed to say, he was "playing to the gallery", which in many Georgian theatres no longer exists. The Talbot scenes in 1 *Henry VI* have an attractive eagerness and lilt and it is no shame to them that, as in the couplets in the first scene of *King Lear* in which the King of France takes the dowerless Cordelia from the too commercial Duke of Burgundy, the note is pitched high. Shakespeare was not so experienced when he wrote these Talbot scenes as when he wrote *King Lear*, but already he knew the effect he wanted and how to attain it, and was assuredly no novice.

While there are good scenes in 1 *Henry VI* it

cannot be called a good play as we have it, nor is it likely that it was a good play in any of its stages. The two which follow it, which we now call 2 and 3 *Henry VI*, despite their bad connecting links with their successors (these being probably omitted when the successors were to be performed the next day) deserve I think more praise than is usually given them, and I hope that Mr Alexander's bold claim for them, as entirely Shakespeare's, will raise their status. Partly, perhaps, because it has always kept a separate name of its own *Richard III* has enjoyed much greater popularity and attention. It is thus all the more satisfactory that Mr Alexander has succeeded better than any of his predecessors in clearing up the difficulties as to the relation of its two texts. His whole book is a fine attempt to bring new light to bear on problems which have been discussed almost to weariness, and if on some points he has reduced me to a benevolent agnosticism rather than made me a thorough convert this does not lessen my belief that he has produced the best contribution to his subject that has yet been made.

SHAKESPEARE'S
HENRY VI & RICHARD III

THE ARGUMENT

Henry VI and *Richard III*, although not admired
to-day, were popular plays with the Elizabethan
public. The first part of *Henry VI*, with the fate of
Talbot, according to Nashe, moved thousands of
enthusiastic spectators to tears; the success of the
third part provoked the jealous criticism of Greene;
tradition has preserved the triumph of Burbage's
Richard III; and Shakespeare himself in the epilogue
to *Henry V*, asking the approval of his audience in the
name of the mighty men whose story he has presented,
recalls the frequent performance of the histories of the
wars of York and Lancaster. Elizabethan stationers
have added further evidence of their favourable re-
ception; they published what texts they could procure
of 2 and 3 *Henry VI* and *Richard III*, knowing there
would be a demand for them. It is these popular
versions which have created the problems that still
give four comparatively unimportant examples of
Shakespeare's work a very special interest for students
of his text.

On 12 March 1594 the publisher, Thomas
Millington, entered for his copy in the Stationers'
Register[1] a play which he issued in Quarto in the
course of the year, with the title, *The First part of the
Contention betwixt the two famous Houses of Yorke and
Lancaster*; in the following year the same publisher
without further entry in the Register printed the
sequel, *The true Tragedie of Richard Duke of Yorke*,

[1] Under the hands of both the wardens.

*as it was sundrie times acted by the Right Honourable
the Earle of Pembrooke his seruants.* No version of
Richard III was printed till 1597, but once published
by Andrew Wise, it went through numerous editions.
Some twenty-five years later, Heminge and Condell,
Shakespeare's friends and first editors, collecting "all
his Comedies, Histories, and Tragedies" in their
Folio edition of 1623, printed versions of these plays
that differ very materially from those published by
Wise and Millington. To account for the differences
is a problem that has long engaged Shakespeare's
editors and commentators; and, although the solution
might be regarded as of concern only to those with a
peculiar interest in textual studies, the theories of
these investigators have now a place in current talk
about Shakespeare.

Most of those who have compared the earlier and
later versions of 2 and 3 *Henry VI* have found them
so apparently arbitrary in their agreement and differences, that they have been able to relate them, only
by supposing that different hands contributed not
merely to the different versions but to different parts
of the same version. This conjecture at once gives
the inquiry a more general interest: it raises the very
important question, Who were Shakespeare's col-
laborators? Malone, the first to ask this question in
an attempt to solve the textual difficulty, thought, to
begin with, that he had a certain clue to the other
dramatists: in the end, although convinced that others
as well as Shakespeare had worked on 2 and 3 *Henry
VI*, he remained uncertain whom exactly to name
from Marlowe, Greene, Peele, or Lodge, or what
exactly to assign to each. Others using the doubtful
evidence which Malone had at last to rely on have

ventured to offer more positive conclusions, some attempting to estimate to a line the share of each collaborator. There is unfortunately no real agreement among the investigators; almost every author of the time who is known to have written for the stage is supposed by one or other to have penned a part in these plays; what the inquiries have in common is the question with which they all start. To this a convincing answer has yet to be found; but the very important assumption prompting the question itself has been generally taken as established.

Once accept Malone's argument that we can solve the textual problem of 2 and 3 *Henry VI* only by recognizing that several authors have contributed to it, and the inference that Heminge and Condell have preserved for us a considerable body of the work of these men is hardly to be avoided. Malone was of this opinion: he thought that the first editors were not particular whose plays they printed provided there was embedded in them something by Shakespeare; he considered he had positive proof of this in 2 and 3 *Henry VI* (and in *The Taming of the Shrew*), and was prepared therefore to allow the more doubtful evidence of style and vocabulary considerable weight in deciding in other pieces what was or was not by Shakespeare. On these grounds he attributed 1 *Henry VI* to others; so much indeed of their work seemed to him preserved there that he concluded the Folio editors retained it merely as an introduction to the two later parts, Shakespeare having added a few lines to link them together. Malone thus provided a foundation for the casual speculation of some of the earlier editors, that Shakespeare had only a small part in certain plays in the Folio.

The liberty of conjecture this assumption gives did not, fortunately, tempt Malone to put aside scholarly method; he checked his own personal impressions whenever possible by reference to traditional or textual evidence; and although it is not the temper of his literary discernment, but his learning, industry and candour, that have made Malone the first among Shakespeare scholars for some things, he made his examination with caution, and ventured fewer rash judgments as a literary assessor than others of more poetic apprehension. Too many coming after him, confident in his assumptions, have shown no such restraint, and through the breach made by Malone has poured a flood of conjecture that threatens to obliterate every familiar landmark. He argued that the circumstances attending Shakespeare's first efforts as dramatist explain why other hands are to be found in the early plays (later work except *Henry VIII* he gave to Shakespeare himself): they are disposed to assume that any work in the Folio which does not bear what seem to them unmistakable marks of Shakespeare's style must be by someone else. Later critics might have paused to consider the strange results such a touchstone would produce applied to the Waverley novels, or the poetry of Wordsworth, or Shelley: here is no lack of that "visible inequality" which so troubled Malone. Although in these later instances criticism cannot set aside the accepted authorship because of the obvious inequality of the work, little doubt is entertained of the value of this criterion in examining the plays in the Folio. How easy and popular its application may be can be seen in the notices which daily and weekly papers sometimes print of Shakespeare productions; the following extracts from an article in *The Observer* (25 January 1925) on *Richard II* show to what a pass the specialist can bring the minds of intelligent laymen.

This play is the work of three people: of Shakespeare, of someone worse than Shakespeare, and of someone as good as, though different from, Shakespeare. (The fact may not have been noticed before.)

The Shakespeare part is easy enough. Some of it is magnificent, some of it is drivel.

Then there is the obviously non-Shakespearian part.

Finally, there are the touches put in by someone who was as good as Shakespeare, but who wasn't Shakespeare— or was Shakespeare in a rare and never-repeated mood. Shakespeare was often a metaphysician, never a theologian, nor, for that matter, a Christian. The ancient world of gods and heroes appealed to him. The Middle Ages had left a few superstitious terrors on his mind. But the figures of Christian mythology and their significance seem utterly to have passed him by. He never refers to them on his own, hardly ever makes mention of them even in the mouths of characters who might be supposed to feel them most strongly. He is alternately believer in Fate, pagan, or agnostic, never for a moment a believer in Christ. But someone who lent a hand in writing *Richard II* was very much a Christian.

It is hard to believe that this writer did not intend to parody a fashionable style in criticism. The idea which he presents us with in the first paragraph as his own invention is designed, like the contrivances the White Knight displayed to Alice, for a situation existing only in the fancy of the inventor. Shakespeare had as much need of a collaborator to insert the biblical allusions in *Richard II*, as horses have of anklets to guard against the bites of sharks. But in the

field of Shakespearean criticism there are more White
Knights than Alice encountered in Wonderland, each
encumbered with a load of the strangest and most
unnecessary suggestions; and the latest invention is
neither better nor worse than many others.

In his work on the life of Shakespeare Dr Smart has
demonstrated how the conviction that Shakespeare's
plays and poems must have been written by Bacon or
some noble Lord is only the humorous exaggeration
of a foolish fancy long entertained even by scholars.
So many of his biographers have represented the poet
as an ignorant youth from a benighted neighbourhood
that the Baconians and others have at last taken their
word for it, and concluded, with some reason, that
this was not the author of *Hamlet* or *Lucrece*. The
invincible doubt, however, with which these critics
oppose the plainest assurances of the poet's contemporaries is now seen as the natural counterpart in their
uncritical minds of their easy credulity in accepting
as unquestionable fact Restoration gossip and guess-
work about Shakespeare's younger days. The
Christian contemporary and collaborator who was as
good a poet as Shakespeare is a worthy rival to the
Lord Chancellor of the Baconians, if he is not merely
another of that versatile man's disguises; his discovery,
however, suggests that in textual as in biographical
studies conjecture so counter to truth has been from
the first on a false trail. A re-examination of the
textual problems in *Henry VI* and *Richard III* affords
an opportunity of judging with what justification
scholars first started the cry in this direction.

In the pages to follow it will be maintained that
The Contention and *Richard Duke of York* afford no
evidence that Heminge and Condell printed the work

of others as Shakespeare's, since these Quartos are not, as Malone argued, early versions worked on by Shakespeare, but only bad versions of 2 and 3 *Henry VI*. Some of the more elaborate bibliographical or textual arguments devised since Malone's time to prove 1, 2, 3 *Henry VI* and *Richard III* in part only by Shakespeare are also examined. So long as Malone's position was regarded as sound, certain of these arguments were not unplausible; the loss of his support, however, leaves them, it is contended, exposed to quite obvious but destructive lines of criticism.

If there is no satisfactory evidence to establish the collaboration of Greene or Marlowe or others with Shakespeare, the suggestion has no further right to consideration, for there is nothing in the circumstances of its origin that enables us to dispense with this necessary proof. Malone was not the first to question Shakespeare's authorship of *Henry VI*, but the early editors were naturally tempted to fill the void in their knowledge by conjecture. Such conjectural history is worthless. Pope is the first to treat the text in the light of what he considered its history, and his views were long quoted with approval by his successors. To him Heminge and Condell were "mere players", the inferiors in every way of "the gentlemen of the stage" of his own day, and their text a fair field in which to exercise his taste; the more so since he recognised that their original copies, as well as those for the Quartos, were in many instances "no better copies than *the prompter's book*"; and these he concluded must have "been cut, or added to, arbitrarily", in a manner that completely disfigured the original. His guesses about the authorship of some of the Folio plays are of the same value as those about the editors and their text: he ventured to declare of some of the plays in the First Folio "(particularly *Love's Labour's Lost*, *The Winter's Tale*, *Comedy of Errors* and *Titus Andronicus*) that only some characters, single scenes, or perhaps a few particular passages" were of Shakespeare's hand.

Shakespeare's fellows, it is now known, were not denied "an intimacy with people of the first condition", being men of substance and intelligence. There is indeed a good story of Burbage, later the leading actor of the Company, told by a man named Bishop, who after a stormy encounter with the young man had cause to complain that "the said Richard Burbage scornfully and disdainfully playing with this deponent's nose" threatened to beat him, "and did challenge the field of him at that time". But this was in the player's fiery youth: in maturer years Burbage occupied his leisure with portrait painting, and was the honoured friend of many of worship, amongst others the Earl of Pembroke. All the evidence points to Shakespeare's Company as a group of sober men living in reputation, and Heminge and Condell as well qualified by their position in the Company, their native wit, and their affection for their friend, to collect his plays for publication.

Had Heminge and Condell shown the same judgment in preparing Shakespeare's plays for the reader as the actors of a later time did in playing them to their audiences, Pope might well have suspected their text. Before the Folio, however, fourteen Good Quartos had been printed, some nearly thirty years earlier, and they provide a sufficient check on Pope's hasty opinion: a comparison between these early versions and those furnished by Heminge and Condell does not disclose the extensive and arbitrary changes Pope's conjecture would lead us to expect. And when Pope complains that the Folio text and that of the Quartos are *no better* than what was found in prompt copies he touches on the very point that modern textual criticism has so decisively turned in their favour: behind many of these prompt copies, there can be no reasonable doubt, is the very authority we look for—the hand of Shakespeare himself.

Pope's conjectures about authorship cannot be separated from those about the editors and their text by supposing that his literary taste was more reliable than his historical knowledge. What plays are Shakespeare's, or what are not, is not a question of taste; and, if it were, a study of the "excessively bad" passages from many of the plays that Pope "degraded to the bottom of the page" as interpolations would not encourage one to believe he could answer it with any certainty. It was a better scholar than Pope and one of sounder historical sense who first denied *Henry VI* to Shakespeare; but Theobald had the same ideas in general about the first editors and their copy as Pope, and this was only another guess. He did indeed mention a few isolated points which suggested the idea to him, but as Johnson observed, and Tyrwhitt concurred, these were no proof whatever of his assertion.

To-day the textual situation is quite different from that in which Theobald hazarded his guess. During two hundred years' study of their text, Heminge and Condell's good faith in dealing with their material has been gradually re-established; and in our own time Professor Pollard has finally cleared them of dishonesty. Those who question their word must now make good their charges; till then we can accept the statements with which they introduced the plays to a reading public, some of whom must have been able to judge whether they were true or false. In their letters they wish that Shakespeare had "ouerseen his owne writings" and regret he was not "exequutor to his own writings" and it is these writings they profess to have collected, referring to the collected works as "his Orphanes", "his playes". For the authorship of two of the plays dealt with in this volume we have fortunately independent and reliable testimony. Those who are prepared to set aside the assertions of the first editors and the evidence of their contemporaries for anything less than clear proof of the contrary, or merely to follow a private fancy, may not venture as far or as confidently as the dramatic critic in *The Observer*, but they are on the same road.

The last chapter includes some very debatable matter about Shakespeare's first or perhaps his second Company. This must in the end be left to the historians of the drama; it forms no essential part of the present argument; it is necessary, however, to guard against the view that the evidence on this point indicates that the young Shakespeare was merely revising the works of Marlowe or Greene or some other. Taken by themselves the entries in Henslowe's *Diary* and the statements on the early Quarto title pages need not imply this, and they can as easily and perhaps more easily be accommodated to a different view. Whether the account of Shakespeare's beginnings as a dramatist found in the following pages or that which it is designed to replace is the more credible must depend, for the present, on the interpretation of the evidence examined in the earlier chapters.

I. GREENE'S QUOTATION FROM
3 *HENRY VI*

SHAKESPEARE'S intimate friends and old associates Heminge and Condell printed 1, 2, 3 *Henry VI* and *Richard III* as his work in their edition of the plays. For *Richard III* there is the independent evidence of Meres, who in his *Palladis Tamia* (1598) included it in a list of twelve of Shakespeare's plays; for 3 *Henry VI* we have Greene's important reference in 1592 which "points at Shakespeare as the author".

Greene's reference to 3 *Henry VI* was recovered for modern students by Thomas Tyrwhitt, who was the first not only to direct the attention of scholars to the punning allusion to Shakespeare, but to point out its true interpretation and bearing on the present problem. He wrote:

Though the objections which have been raised [by Theobald and Warburton] to the genuineness of the three plays of Henry the Sixth have been fully considered and answered by Dr Johnson, it may not be amiss to add here, from a contemporary writer, a passage, which...points at Shakespeare as the author of them. (Boswell's *Malone*, XVIII, 551.)

Tyrwhitt's conclusion that Shakespeare is pointed at as their author is the natural and indeed the only interpretation which the passage will bear; but it has been used to prove the very opposite of what it implies, and Malone calls it the chief hinge of his argument that 2 and 3 *Henry VI* are largely from other hands than Shakespeare's. As his interpreta-

tion, though erroneous, has been very widely received, it is necessary to quote and examine the
passage in some detail.

Greene made his attack on Shakespeare in a
pamphlet which he wrote as he was dying, and which
was published after his death. The title explains the
contents:

> *Greenes, Groats-worth of witte, bought with a million of*
> *Repentance. Describing the follie of youth, the falshood of*
> *make-shifte flatterers, the miserie of the negligent, and mis-*
> *chiefes of deceiuing Courtezans. Written before his death*
> *and published at his dyeing request.*

In this work Greene inserted a letter headed:

> *To those Gentlemen his Quondam acquaintance, that*
> *spend their wits in making plaies, R. G. wisheth a better*
> *exercise, and wisdome to preuent his extremities.*

As well as censuring the occupation of the dramatists,
he abuses the players they write for, and especially
Shakespeare.

Greene professes to warn his former acquaintances
against so precarious a livelihood as play-making, by
asking them to learn from his misfortunes how such
a career leads to destitution. He begins however by
charging the first he addresses with some of the many
sins that he acknowledges have brought his own unhappy end upon him; "I knowe the least of my
demerits merit this miserable death", he confesses,
and then exhorts the other to reform his life. As
Greene comes to each in turn he provides a clue to
his identity. The "famous gracer of Tragedians",
with whom he begins and whom he accuses of
atheism, is undoubtedly Marlowe; but the second,
"yong *Iuuenall*, that byting Satyrist, that lastly with

mee together writ a Comedie", is variously taken as
Lodge, or Nashe; the phrase "by sweet S. George"
may point to Peele as the third, since his Christian
name was George. Marlowe was accused not only of
atheism, but of some other sin all reference to which,
however, Chettle, who prepared the work for the press,
excised, since "to publish it was intollerable"; the
second is reproved for his satirical licence; the third
is guilty of making his living by writing plays, and
relying on the support of such base fellows as players.

When speaking to Peele, Greene introduces an
attack on the actors who have, he declares, deserted
him so basely in his financial and bodily distress.
"Thou art", he says, "unworthy better hap, sith
thou dependest on so meane a stay", and then gives
this warning to them all:

> Base minded men all three of you, if by my miserie you
> be not warnd: for unto none of you (like mee) sought those
> burres to cleaue: those Puppets (I meane) that spake from
> our mouths, those Anticks garnisht in our colours. Is it not
> strange, that I, to whom they all haue beene beholding: is it
> not like that you, to whome they all haue beene beholding,
> shall (were yee in that case as I am now) bee both at once of
> them forsaken? Yes trust them not: for there is an upstart
> Crow, beautified with our feathers, that with his *Tygers
> hart wrapt in a Players hyde,* supposes he is as well able to
> bombast out a blanke verse as the best of you: and beeing
> an absolute *Iohannes fac totum,* is in his owne conceit the
> onely Shake-scene in a countrey.... whilest you may, seeke
> you better Maisters; for it is pittie men of such rare wits,
> should be subiect to the pleasure of such rude groomes.
> (G. B. Harrison's reprint of 1592 ed., 45.)

This warning against the ingratitude of actors should
be taken, he adds, not only by the three acquaintances

already mentioned, but by two more whom he knows, and by those many others he does not know who will in the future venture on the fatal profession of play-making.

In this I might insert two more, that both haue writ against these buckram Gentlemen: but lette their owne workes serue to witnesse against their owne wickednesse, if they perseuere to maintaine any more such peasants. For other new-commers, I leaue them to the mercie of these painted monsters, who (I doubt not) will driue the best minded to despise them: for the rest, it skils not though they make a ieast at them.

The letter ends with some good advice to the three first mentioned:

Delight not (as I have done) in irreligious oathes.... Despise drunkennes.... Flie lust.... Abhorre those Epicures, whose loose life hath made religion lothsome to your eares... for mans time is not of it selfe so short, but it is more shortned by sinne.

As before, Greene passes abruptly from his warning against sin to a warning against players.

The fire of my light is now at the last snuffe, and for want of wherewith to sustaine it, there is no substance lefte for life to feede on. Trust not then (I beseech ye) to such weake staies: for they are as changeable in minde, as in many attyres. Wel, my hand is tyrde, and I am forst to leaue where I would begin: for a whole booke cannot containe their wrongs, which I am forst to knit up in some fewe lines of words. *Desirous that you should liue, though himselfe be dying:* Robert Greene.

This is a pathetic document, and it is unnecessary to criticize its incoherence, or the strange connection between the wages of sin and the payments of the

actors. Greene had a long standing grievance against
actors, and had already in 1590, in his *Never too Late*,
complained that the performer, who merely repeats
the lines of an abler brain, makes far more than the
author; and he addressed one individual in terms
which are very similar to those employed in the letter:

Why *Roscius*, art thou proud with *Esops* Crow, being
pranct with the glorie of others feathers? of thy selfe thou
canst say nothing, and if the Cobler hath taught thee to
say *Aue Caesar*, disdain not thy tutor, because thou pratest
in a Kings chamber.

Of thyself thou canst say nothing, is the sting in his
jibe at the player who may indeed play in the royal
presence, and receive honour and reward for his
performance: he has only been repeating what the
author has written for him. This is still the burden
of the later complaint; here the actors are called
"those Puppets that spake from our mouths, those
Anticks garnisht in our colours". His argument at
this point may be reworded for clearness. If these
puppets have forsaken me with whom they once so
closely associated for their own profit, they will be
much readier to forsake you to whom they never
sought to cleave. Just as it is strange that I to whom
they owe so much, so it is likely that you to whom
they owe so much, should, both of us, be forsaken by
them. "Both" in Greene's sentence does not refer
to two persons, as some have supposed, but to the two
subjects of the verb forsaken—Greene on the one
hand and his three friends on the other. And the
actors have this further inducement for dispensing
with their services: there is an actor, one like Roscius
proud with Aesop's crow being prankt with the

glory of others feathers, here described as "an up-start Crow, beautified with our feathers", who, not content to masquerade in the borrowed plumage which all his kind enjoy, ventures to imitate the very voice of his betters; he "supposes he is as well able to bombast out a blanke verse as the best". The players Greene implies will naturally prefer the work of one of their own tribe.

The jibe that Shakespeare was "an upstart Crow, beautified with our feathers" has been taken to mean that he had been guilty of appropriating the work of Greene and his acquaintances, and incorporating it in his own dramatic compositions; but this phrase has exactly the same meaning as the words Greene applies to "Roscius": one is proud with Aesop's crow being prankt with the glory of others' feathers, the other is an upstart crow beautified with our feathers. Against the actor there is no charge of literary theft. He does indeed when acting take profit and applause which Greene thought by rights due to the author, but he is not a plagiarist. He is however an actor, and that is offence enough for Greene, for all actors are upstart crows beautified with the feathers of the dramatists. The phrase used of Shakespeare only points to him as that opprobrious thing to Greene, an actor.

Greene emphasizes the fact that Shakespeare is an actor, so that the enormity of what follows may produce its proper effect. This puppet so far from recognizing that he is by his very calling an upstart has further ambitions: he ventures to compose for himself, and thinks that the fustian he produces can compare with the verse of men like Marlowe. Greene was scornful before of the player who could of himself say nothing, but the spectacle of a player speaking for himself turns his scorn to bitterest gall. To show what may be expected from such a quarter, Greene invites his readers to laugh at the style of the upstart crow by parodying one of his striking lines. The line is from 3 *Henry VI* (Act I, sc. iv), where York, a prisoner and about to be killed by his enemies, addresses Queen Margaret in a speech beginning,

She-wolf of France but worse than wolves of France,

and which includes the line,

O tiger's heart wrapp'd in a woman's hide!

This line is derided in Greene's deliberate misquotation as the kind of stuff produced by the man who thinks himself the only Shake-scene in the country.

In the whole indictment there is no word of plagiarism. Had Shakespeare used Greene's material this charge would have been pushed home without hesitation. It is sometimes stated that when a play was purchased by a company they could alter it as they liked; that had Shakespeare done so much for his Company to a play by Greene he was within the law, however annoyed Greene might have felt. But there is no clear example of a play written by one man being added to during the author's lifetime by another of respectable standing who was not his friend or collaborator; and, further, the existence of such a custom would not have prevented Greene, any more than it has some later commentators, denouncing it in unmistakable terms as unfair. But the only two accusations made against Shakespeare are that he was an actor, "an upstart Crow", and that being this he yet ventured to write plays. There is little logic in Greene's case, but he was a disappointed and bitter man; and the bitterness of the attack need not suggest to us that it could only have been inspired by what he considered the theft of his literary reputation. The contents of his purse were unfortunately of much more importance to Greene, at this moment, than his good name as a writer, and it was the loss of his daily bread that he laid at the door of the actors. Shakespeare's popularity as a writer he regarded in his bitterness as merely an aggravation of this wrong; his competition had increased the difficulty of making a living, and Greene wished to be revenged on him and the whole pack of players.

This interpretation of Greene's reference to Shakespeare is only an expansion of that first given by Tyrwhitt. He refers to Greene's letter as an "address to his brother poets, to dissuade them from writing any more for the stage, on account of the ill treatment which they were used to receive from the players". After quoting the attack he continues, "there can be no doubt, I think, that *Shake-scene* alludes to Shakespeare; or that *his tygres heart wrapt in a players hyde* is a parodie upon the line of York's speech to Margaret", in 3 *Henry VI*. Tyrwhitt concluded therefore that Shakespeare was the writer of the line so parodied. So much is certain; and his further conclusion that Shakespeare must be regarded as the author of the play from which Greene quotes cannot be rejected, unless there is unmistakable evidence to the contrary. Indeed, as Tyrwhitt says, the quotation supports the ascription of the three parts of *Henry VI* to Shakespeare.

Malone, who took over this passage from Tyrwhitt, interpreted it in an entirely opposite sense. In his dissertation on the three parts of *Henry VI*, "tending to show that those Plays were not written originally by Shakespeare", he says:

the passage quoted by Mr Tyrwhitt...affords decisive support to the hypothesis that I am endeavouring to maintain; which, indeed, that pamphlet first suggested to me... this passage is the chief hinge of my argument.

But to make the passage bear the meaning he requires of it he has to give the two decisive phrases of the letter a forced and clearly erroneous interpretation.

"What does the writer mean by calling Shakespeare 'a crow beautified with our feathers'?" Malone asks, and replies:

My solution is, that Greene and Peele were the joint authors of the two quarto plays, or that Greene was the author of one and Peele of the other.... Greene could not conceal the mortification that he felt at his own fame and that of his associate, both of them old and admired playwrights, being eclipsed by a new *upstart* writer, (for so he calls our great poet,) who had then first, perhaps, attracted the notice of the publick by exhibiting two plays, formed upon old dramas written by them, considerably enlarged and improved.

But Greene did not call Shakespeare an upstart writer, he calls him an "upstart Crow", and this need mean no more than an actor: that this was his meaning is made very probable by the similar phrase he uses of the actor "Roscius"; that Malone's reading of the phrase cannot be right is made certain by the fact that it involves him in an obviously absurd and ungrammatical interpretation of what follows.

Of the second phrase, "with his *Tygers hart wrapt in a Players hyde*", Malone says:

Greene wishing to depreciate our author, very naturally

quotes a line from one of the pieces which Shakespeare had thus *re-written.*....This line, with many others, Shake-peare adopted without any alteration.

But is it natural for Greene to claim a line as his own or his friend's by quoting it in a distorted form? This is an unusual and unintelligible proceeding. Further to give the passage this meaning Malone ignores the force which attaches in English to the use of *his* before such a depreciatory quotation: this use of *his* indicates that the victim is being condemned out of his own mouth. Bardell *v.* Pickwick furnishes a suitable precedent to follow in an examination of Greene's phrase.[1] When Mr Serjeant Buzfuz in addressing the jury said, "Pickwick...comes before you today with his heartless tomato sauce and warming pans", that intelligent dozen of men knew he was referring to the covert communications in the defendant's handwriting which had just been read in court; the incriminating words are quoted from the first letter, "Dear Mrs B.— Chops and Tomato sauce. Yours, Pickwick", and from the very remarkable expression which concluded the second, "Dont trouble yourself about the warming-pan". Counsel pins the words to Pickwick by this pointed use of "his". Greene is possibly even more ingenious than the Serjeant in selecting his quotation, which glances not only at Shakespeare's private character, but at his public profession, as well as his pretensions as a dramatist; but the method is the same: Greene would persuade us that Shakespeare's own words betray him, and that

---

[1] *Shakespeare: Truth and Tradition,* by John S. Smart, p. 195, gives many more examples. The quotation in the text was suggested to me by Dr Smart himself a few days before his death.

his despicable verse is the best evidence of the vanity of his ambition. The line therefore which Greene introduces by "his" cannot in its original form be other than Shakespeare's.

At a later date Malone was prepared to modify his interpretation of this passage but only in unessentials; he still continued to regard it as evidence that 3 *Henry VI* contained the work of other men than Shakespeare, but suggested Marlowe instead of Greene or Peele as the author of the old play. This change did not enable him to explain with any greater plausibility Greene's quotation; it only increased the confusion in his interpretation. He continued unaware of the real error in his reading of Greene's words, being distracted by another consideration.

The line Greene parodied,

> O tiger's heart wrapp'd in a woman's hide!

Malone found in *Richard Duke of York* as well as in 3 *Henry VI* itself. He had convinced himself that the Quarto was an old play in which Shakespeare had no part, and was satisfied therefore that the line could not be by Shakespeare. His thoughts set in this direction, he overlooked the obvious point of Greene's words, although the meaning had already been pointed out by Tyrwhitt.

But Malone's assumption that *The Contention* and *Richard Duke of York* are old plays, or earlier than the Folio versions of 2 and 3 *Henry VI*, can be shown to be without foundation. The textual evidence proves that they are later productions than Shakespeare's, and there remains no excuse for continuing to accept Malone's complete misinterpretation of Greene's letter. It must be rejected as not only in contradiction to Greene's very words, but as framed to agree with what are only Malone's false assumptions. If Malone can be proved in error about the Quartos of 2 and 3 *Henry VI*, the letter is evidence that, like Heminge and Condell, Greene regarded 3 *Henry VI* as a work by Shakespeare.

II. THE BAD QUARTOS OF
2 AND 3 *HENRY VI*

IN the course of his commentary on 2 and 3
Henry VI, Malone regularly directs the attention
of his reader to those passages in the Quartos
which are not to be found in the Folio, or which
contain different circumstances, names, or phrases,
from the parallel passages in Shakespeare's version:
these variations he regarded as sufficient evidence
that the Quartos could not be surreptitious copies
derived from the Folio text. His argument is sum-
marized in a typical note to 2 *Henry VI*, Act iii,
sc. i, ll. 282–4:

Enter a Poste.

Post.   Great Lords, from Ireland am I come amaine,
            To signifie, that Rebels there are up,
            And put the Englishmen unto the Sword.

After quoting the very different version in *The
Contention,*

Messen. Madame, I bring you newes from Ireland,
            The wilde Onele my Lords, is up in Armes,
            With troupes of Irish Kernes that uncontrold,
            Doth plant themselues within the English pale.

Malone continues,

Surely here is not an imperfect exhibition of the lines in
the folio, hastily taken down in the theatre by the ear or
in shorthand....We have here an original and distinct
draught; so that we must be obliged to maintain that
Shakespeare wrote *two* plays on the present subject, a
hasty sketch, and a more finished performance; or else must

acknowledge that he formed the piece before us on a foundation laid by another writer.

He draws a similar conclusion from the divergence of the Quarto from the Folio at Act I, sc. iii, l. 211, when he asks, "what spurious copy, or imperfect transcript taken in short-hand, ever produced such variations as these?"

It must be admitted that as long as *The Contention* and *Richard Duke of York* are regarded as spurious copies produced by shorthand writers Malone's repeated questions are difficult to answer; but a note by Steevens might have warned him, or at least subsequent commentators, that his views on the nature of spurious copy were too narrow, because he ignored certain obvious and well-established practices in the business of the theatres. To Malone's question at Act I, sc. iii, Steevens replied:

> Such varieties, during several years, were to be found in every MS copy of Mr Sheridan's then unprinted *Duenna*, as used in country theatres. The dialogue of it was obtained piece-meal, and connected by frequent interpolations.

Steevens however never followed up this line of criticism, and was betrayed into supporting Malone by a not uncommon desire to be in the right whatever the event. While consistently opposing his argument in detail he permitted himself to sum up the question in debate by observing:

> if he (Malone) proves anything, it is a position hazarded by me long ago; viz. that our author had as much hand in the present dramas, as in several others that pass under his name....that Shakespeare did not attempt a single play on any subject, till the effect of the same story, or at least the ruling incidents in it, had been tried on the stage, and familiarised to his audience.

This ability to swear in both the scales against either scale naturally exposed Steevens to the charge of equivocation, and the justness of his criticism of Malone was obscured by the excess of his ingenuity. Later critics have referred to the conditions that often obtained in country theatres in explaining the origin and nature of surreptitious copies of plays; and the recent inquiry by Mr Crompton Rhodes into the text of Sheridan's *Duenna* and *The School for Scandal* has not only yielded brilliant results for the text of Sheridan, it has demonstrated that Steeven's observation is a sufficient answer to Malone's argument and provides the true solution of the difficulty.

(i) Theatrical Piracy

Although Sheridan was working almost two hundred years later than Shakespeare the legal means which he had at his disposal for preventing unauthorized provincial performances had not improved. His early comedy *The Rivals* was printed soon after its appearance on the London stage, and the text was frequently used at provincial theatres without the author's sanction. It is easy therefore to understand why he did not hurry to print his later works, *The Duenna* and *The School for Scandal*: he had to adopt the same defence as Shakespeare and his company. And the interest for Shakespeare students in Mr Rhodes's investigation is that he can show in considerable detail how this refusal to print was countered by the theatrical pirates of Sheridan's day. Although authorized texts of *The Duenna* and *The School for Scandal* were not published till nearly twenty years after their first performance in London, pirated versions were being regularly played in the provinces, and frequently printed long before the true copies appeared. It is now established that some of these garbled versions are extant and that the methods employed in their construction are recorded in contemporary documents. As the conditions under which these texts were produced did not differ in any important circumstance from those of earlier times, Mr Rhodes has provided important evidence which can be used in controlling deductions made from the text of bad Elizabethan Quartos.

The truth of Steevens' observation can now be tested by comparing a passage from *The Duenna* with the version in a provincial piracy. Sheridan's text comes first.

I.   Louisa's *Dressing-Room.*
                Enter Maid *and* Isaac.

Maid. Sir, my mistress will wait on you presently.
                                        [*Goes to the door.*]

Isaac. When she's at leisure—dont hurry her—
[*Mendoza.*]   [*Exit* Maid.]
            I wish I had ever practised a love-scene—
            I doubt I shall make a poor figure—I couldn't
            be more afraid if I was going before the
            Inquisition—so! the door opens—yes, she's
            coming—the very rustling of her silk has a
            disdainful sound.

II.   Chamber.
En[*och* Hark! I thought I heard her!...No; it was
Issachar.] only my fears!...Lord! she must be a most
            beautiful and enchanting creature!...I think
            I hear the rattling of silks:...it must be she.
            ...O, here she comes.

No one doubts that this paraphrase which was passed off on the public is later than Sheridan's own version; the additions and interpolations therefore offer no serious problem to those who regard Sheridan as the author of *The Duenna*. The variations from the Folio in *The Contention* and *Richard Duke of York*, which so occupied Malone, need raise no greater difficulty about the question of authorship and revision than those in the texts of *The Duenna*— once it is clearly established that the Quartos are piracies. It is to be expected that in a piracy a poor report would be eked out with additions and interpolations; and unless those in *The Contention* and *Richard Duke of York* can be shown to be beyond the power of a pirate, what Malone has offered as evidence of the originality of the Quarto texts is only additional proof that they are derivative and degraded versions.

There can be no question fortunately about the nature of important parts of the Quarto texts. The dialogue of *The Contention* reveals the hand of the pirate in one of the indispensable scenes in the play. In 2 *Henry VI*, Act ii, sc. ii, the dramatist presents York's pretext for claiming the crown from the Lancastrian king. This is necessary to make clear the details of the Wars of the Roses; and the Duke's speech which sets forth his claim that he is nearer in descent to Edward III than Henry, and so has a better right to the throne, is the key to the rest of the drama. Shakespeare treats the question with the precision of the chroniclers. To see how limpingly the Quarto writer halts after Shakespeare one has only to compare the two versions in which this necessary question is considered.

I.   The Contention (1594)

Enter the Duke of *Yorke*, and the Earles of
Salsbury and *Warwicke*.

Yorke. My Lords our simple supper ended, thus,
Let me reueale vnto your honours here,
The right and title of the house of Yorke,
To Englands Crowne by liniall desent.
  War. Then Yorke begin, and if thy claime be good,
The Neuils are thy subiects to command.
  Yorke. Then thus my Lords.
Edward the third had seuen sonnes,
The first was Edward the blacke Prince,
Prince of Wales.
The second was Edmund of Langly,
Duke of Yorke. ·
The third was Lyonell Duke of Clarence.
The fourth was Iohn of Gaunt,
The Duke of Lancaster.
The fifth was Roger Mortemor, Earle of March.
The sixt was sir Thomas of Woodstocke.
William of Winsore was the seuenth and last.
Now, Edward the black Prince he died before his father, and left
behinde him Richard, that afterwards was King, Crownde by
the name of Richard the second, and he died without an heire.
Edmund of Langly Duke of Yorke died, and left behind him two
daughters, Anne and Elinor.
Lyonell Duke of Clarence died, and left behinde Alice, Anne,
and Elinor, that was after married to my father, and by her I
claime the Crowne, as the true heire to Lyonell Duke

II.   The second Part of Henry the Sixt (1623)
             Enter Yorke, Salisbury, and Warwick.

Yorke. Now my good Lords of Salisbury & Warwick,
Our simple Supper ended, giue me leaue,
In this close Walke, to satisfie my selfe,
In crauing your opinion of my Title,
Which is infallible, to Englands Crowne.
Salisb. My Lord, I long to heare it at full.
Warw. Sweet *Yorke* begin: and if thy clayme be good,
The *Neuills* are thy Subiects to command.
Yorke. Then thus:
Edward the third, my Lords, had seuen Sonnes:
The first, *Edward* the Black-Prince, Prince of Wales;
The second, *William* of Hatfield; and the third,
Lionel, Duke of Clarence; next to whom,
Was *Iohn* of Gaunt, the Duke of Lancaster;
The fift, was *Edmond Langley,* Duke of Yorke;
The sixt, was *Thomas* of Woodstock, Duke of Gloster;
William of Windsor was the seuenth, and last.
Edward the Black-Prince dyed before his Father,
And left behinde him *Richard,* his onely Sonne,
Who after *Edward* the third's death, raign'd as King,
Till *Henry Bullingbrooke,* Duke of Lancaster,
The eldest Sonne and Heire of *Iohn* of Gaunt,
Crown'd by the Name of *Henry* the fourth,
Seiz'd on the Realme, depos'd the rightfull King,
Sent his poore Queene to France from whence she came,
And him to Pumfret; where, as all you know,
Harmlesse *Richard* was murthered traiterously.
Warw. Father, the Duke hath told the truth;
Thus got the House of *Lancaster* the Crowne.
Yorke. Which now they hold by force, and not by right:
For *Richard,* the first Sonnes Heire, being dead,
The Issue of the next Sonne should haue reign'd.
Salisb. But *William* of Hatfield dyed without an
Heire.

of Clarence, the third sonne to Edward the third. Now sir. In the time of Richards raigne, Henry of Bullingbrooke, sonne and heire to Iohn of Gaunt, the Duke of Lancaster fourth sonne to Edward the third, he claimde the Crowne, deposde the Merthfull King, and as both you know, in Pomphret Castle harmelesse Richard was shamefully murthered, and so by Richards death came the house of Lancaster unto the Crowne.

Sals. Sauing your tale my Lord, as I haue heard, in the raigne of Bullenbrooke, the Duke of Yorke did claime the Crowne, and but for Owin Glendor, had bene King.

Yorke. True. But so it fortuned then, by meanes of that monstrous rebel Glendor, the noble Duk of York was done to death, and so euer since the heires of Iohn of Gaunt haue possessed the Crowne. But if the issue of the elder should sucseed before the issue of the yonger, then am I lawfull heire unto the kingdome.

Warwicke. What plaine proceedings can be more plaine, hee claimes it from Lyonel Duke of Clarence, the third sonne to Edward the third, and Henry from Iohn of Gaunt the fourth sonne. So that till Lyonels issue failes, his should not raigne. It failes not yet, but florisheth in thee & in thy sons, braue slips of such a stock. Then noble father, kneele we both togither, and in this priuate place, be we the first to honor him with birthright to the Crown.

Yorke. The third Sonne, Duke of Clarence,
From whose Line I clayme the Crowne,
Had Issue *Phillip*, a Daughter,
Who marryed *Edmond Mortimer*, Earle of March:
Edmond had Issue, *Roger*, Earle of March;
Roger had Issue, *Edmond*, *Anne*, and *Elianor*.
    Salisb. This *Edmond*, in the Reigne of *Bullingbrooke*,
As I haue read, layd clayme vnto the Crowne,
And but for *Owen Glendour*, had beene King;
Who kept him in Captiuitie, till he dyed.
But, to the rest.
    Yorke. His eldest Sister, *Anne*,
My Mother, being Heire vnto the Crowne,
Marryed *Richard*, Earle of Cambridge,
Who was to *Edmond Langley*,
Edward the thirds fift Sonnes Sonne;
By her I clayme the Kingdome:
She was Heire to *Roger*, Earle of March,
Who was the Sonne of *Edmond Mortimer*,
Who marryed *Phillip*, sole Daughter
Unto *Lionel*, Duke of Clarence.
So, if the Issue of the elder Sonne
Succeed before the younger, I am King.
    Warw. What plaine proceedings is more plain then this?
Henry doth clayme the Crowne from *Iohn* of Gaunt,
The fourth Sonne, *Yorke* claymes it from the third:
Till *Lionels* Issue fayles, his should not reigne.
It fayles not yet, but flourishes in thee,
And in thy Sonnes, faire slippes of such a Stock.

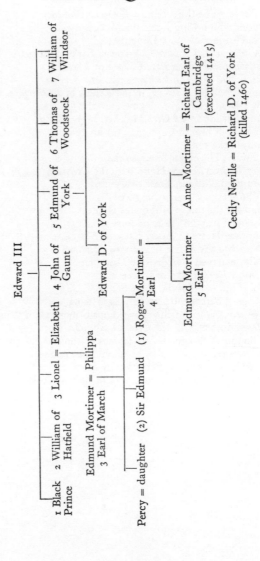

If the account which the Quarto gives of York's descent is checked from the genealogical table on the opposite page, it will be seen that it contains at least five obvious errors. It asserts (i) that Edmund Langley, Duke of York, was Edward III's second son (he was the fifth son), (ii) that Roger Mortimer, Earl of March, was fifth son (he was one of Edward III's great grandsons), (iii) that Edmund Langley left two daughters, Anne and Eleanor (he had two sons and a daughter Constance), (iv) that Lionel, Duke of Clarence, had daughters Alice, Anne, and Eleanor (he had an only daughter Philippa), (v) that York's father, Richard, married one of Lionel's daughters (he married Anne Mortimer, Lionel's great granddaughter). In addition York is made to say that in the reign of Henry IV his ancestor the Duke of York claimed the crown but was done to death by the rebel Glendower. This is also without historical foundation, but while Shakespeare presents all the other points accurately he too stumbles here in saying that Edmund, fifth Earl of March, claimed the crown in the time of Bolingbroke and would have been king but for his imprisonment by Glendower. The first part however of this statement he found in Holinshed, who represents the Duke of York as saying:

Edmund earle of March, my most welbeloued uncle, in the time of the first usurper, (in deed, but not by right, called King Henrie the fourth,) by his coosines the earl of Northumberland, and the lord Persie, (he being then in captiuitie with Owen Glendouer the rebell in Wales,) made his title and righteous claime to the destruction of both the noble persons.

As the table of descent indicates, Holinshed has

confused Edmund Mortimer the fifth Earl with his
father's brother Sir Edmund, who was captured by
Glendower and married to his daughter. Halle and
Holinshed, who reproduces much of Halle, make this
error repeatedly, and Shakespeare following their
chronicles naturally falls into the same confusion.
He introduces it into this scene in 2 *Henry VI*, and
several years later makes the historical plot of 1 *Henry
IV* depend on the same identification of Sir Edmund
and his nephew. The second part of the statement,
that Glendower kept Mortimer a prisoner till his
death, arises from Shakespeare's further confusion of
Sir Edmund with another of Glendower's sons-in-
law. Lord Grey was married to another of Glendower's daughters, and he, according to Halle, was
treated in this manner. Shakespeare's sources explain
his errors; but what account can be given of the
many blunders in the Quarto?

We cannot say that the Quarto was written by a
dramatist who had studied the chronicles, but who
trusted to his memory when he came to composition
and in his impatience confused the details: it is not
merely the details that are incorrect; the argument
in the Quarto taken as a whole has no point whatever. York had to prove that, although descended
from the fifth son of Edward III, he was, because of
his father's marriage with a descendant of the third
son, more in the direct line of succession than the
heirs of the fourth son. The Quarto writer by making
him declare his ancestor the Duke of York to be
second son to Edward III renders further argument
superfluous; he had now no need to claim the throne
through a daughter of the third son as he proceeds
to do. When therefore we come to inquire where he

found, with the other details of his information, the statements that the Duke of York had two daughters Anne and Eleanor, and that Lionel also had daughters called Anne and Eleanor, we need not search for any historical source: a glance at the Folio makes it clear that this repetition was prompted by a confused recollection that

> Roger had issue Edmund, Anne and Eleanor.

All the hopeless confusion in the details of the pedigree and the mechanical repetition of phrases found in the Folio indicate that we have in the Quarto nothing more than someone's attempt to reconstruct from memory one of Shakespeare's scenes. Nor is this peculiarity found only in *The Contention.* The evidence that parts of *Richard Duke of York* are similarly constructed is as decisive.

In 3 *Henry VI*, Act iv, sc. i, Richard and Clarence reproach Edward with preferring his wife's relations before his brothers. Shakespeare found the substance of their complaint in Halle, who reports Clarence's saying to Warwick:

> This you knowe well enough, that the heire of the Lorde Scales he hath maried to his wifes brother, the heire also of the lord Bonuile and Haryngton he hath geuen to his wifes sonne, and theire of the lorde Hungerford he hath graunted to the lorde Hastynges: thre mariages more meter for hys two brethren and kynne then for suche newe foundlynges as he hath bestowed theim on.

The Folio follows this statement, the three heiresses being assigned to Hastings, the Queen's brother, and the Queen's son respectively.

> *Clar.* For this one speech, Lord *Hastings* well deserues
> To haue the Heire of the Lord *Hungerford.*

Rich. And yet me thinks, your Grace hath not done well,
　　　To giue the Heire and Daughter of Lord *Scales*
　　　Unto the Brother of your louing Bride;
　　　Shee better would haue fitted me, or *Clarence*:
　　　But in your Bride you burie Brotherhood.
Clar. Or else you would not haue bestow'd the Heire
　　　Of the Lord *Bonuill* on your new Wiues Sonne.

But the Quarto gives a sadly mangled version of these transactions, asserting that Lord Scales married the daughter of a nobleman described as Lord Bonfield.

Cla. For this one speech the Lord *Hastings* wel deserues,
　　　To haue the daughter and heire of the Lord *Hunger-*
　　　　ford.
　　　. . . . . . .　　. . . . . . .
Cla. I, and for such a thing too the Lord *Scales*
　　　Did well deserue at your hands, to haue the
　　　Daughter of the Lord *Bonfield*, and left your
　　　Brothers go seeke elsewhere, but in
　　　Your madnes, you burie brotherhood.

The point of the matter was that it was the daughter of Lord Scales, not Lord Scales himself, who was involved, and that the male party to the bargain was nearly related to the Queen, and that Lord Bonvill's daughter was given to another of her relatives. The Quarto version mangles history, and has no point of its own.

Any theory that requires us to consider these Quarto scenes as the original composition of Marlowe, Greene, Peele, or Lodge, or indeed anyone who was writing independently, may be dismissed without further consideration. Nor can we attribute their corrupt condition to a compositor, or transcriber, or abridger, or to their combined efforts; to account for it we require to postulate a factor not found in the normal method of transmission. Whoever supplied this portion of the copy for the Quarto had to rely on his memory as no transcriber or printer would find it necessary to do: his confusion has betrayed to us his necessity. Here at least we are dealing not with a transcript of Shakespeare's (or any other writer's) original, but only with a report of that original.

The term "reporting" is not however used here in the restricted sense in which Malone employs it. He thought only of a version written down in shorthand by someone among the audience. But this is only one kind of "report". The essential difference for textual study between a "report" of a play and a "transcript" or version which has reached print in the normal course has been indicated by Dr Greg in his "*Alcazar* and *Orlando*", and consists in this, that one link in the chain which connects the author's manuscript with the report is the memory of one or more persons. In transcription or printing the scribe or printer has to carry words or phrases in his memory, but he compares his work with a version before him to which he can constantly refer. At the critical stage in the preparation of a report this check is absent. The shorthand reporter has to take down what the memories of the actors recall as they deliver their parts, and he cannot compare their version with the authentic words of the author. It is true there is the further difficulty that the actors only deliver their parts once during a performance, and the reporter cannot guarantee that he has reported with perfect accuracy what he has heard; this, however, can be rectified to some extent at subsequent performances, and if the reporter has any skill at all he will at the first trial have caught at least the general drift of the speeches and the order of the ideas and events presented to him. A shorthand report therefore is not a "report" because it is taken down to dictation, as it were, but because it depends ultimately for its accuracy on whether the actors have been faithful to their parts. The errors due to defective hearing and unskilful recording on the part of the shorthand writer must be kept as clearly distinct as possible from those which arise from the entirely different cause of defective memory or the deliberate improvisation of the actors.

Since the characteristic feature of a report is what may be called the memory link, it is clear that if an actor were himself (because his part was missing) to write down his speeches from memory the resulting version would be as much a report as any shorthand record of what he had spoken on the stage. Both would ultimately depend on the memory of the actor.

It is necessary to keep these distinctions in mind as the analysis of passages in *The Contention* and *Richard Duke of York* establishes beyond question that part of these Quartos are reconstructed from memory. Against this evidence Malone's argument that the Quartos contain additions and interpolations has no weight whatever. But although he does nothing to rebut the main conclusion that the Quartos are in part at least reports, his objections help to establish the particular kind of report presented. Malone felt certain that they were not shorthand reports. Further analysis shows that the evidence for this conclusion is adequate. Shorthand reporting that could not attain to greater accuracy than is found in the passages

already examined would be less to be feared as a
method of piracy than a plain attempt in longhand
or a draft from memory; and the inequality between
the parts that even such a short scene as that from
The Contention exhibits, the transposition of phrases
from one place to another, and finally the additional
material not found and, it may safely be said, never
present in the original, definitely rule out this explanation. If shorthand reporting is to be maintained,
these irregularities must be attributed almost wholly
to the faulty delivery of the actors; for no shorthand
reporter could for one thing confuse phrases that lie
scenes apart (and this is often found in the Quartos)
unless they were delivered to him in this manner.
These confusions can only arise in the memory of those
who know the play, or parts in the play, as a whole.

It is in this modified form, however, that shorthand
has been proposed again very recently[1] as an explanation of certain of the well-established Bad
Quartos; the additions and transpositions they contain are attributed to the defective delivery of their
parts by the actors whom the reporter has more or less
faithfully followed. Inequalities are further increased,
it is said, because some actors no doubt spoke more
plainly than others, and because the voice even of an
individual would naturally vary in different situations.
These are conjectures to which it is difficult to
prescribe bounds, but it is certain that they have been
carried far beyond probability when *Hamlet* Q 1 is
offered as a reasonably accurate report of what the
Chamberlain's men made, when acting, of the play
preserved in Q 2 and the Folio. It is clear that the

[1] *The Text of Shakespeare's Hamlet*, by B. A. P. Van Dam,
M.D., Chapter I.

instructions of Hamlet were not meant for actors of this level of incapacity; and that Rosencrantz and Guildenstern might well have smiled at the lenten entertainment in store for the players if they could have done no better than this. But the famous digression on acting suggests that Shakespeare and his fellows would have regarded such an opinion of their care and capacity as monstrous; and till there is positive proof, the theory must be rejected which implies that in the most brilliant age of English drama the leading company in the land were so utterly incompetent. The assumption is the less called for since there are alternative methods of reporting whose practice can be established, not merely from the guesses of one of the victims, but from the statements of the pirates themselves— methods which explain the phenomena of some of the Bad Quartos[1] very much more simply than short-hand reporting.

It is here that the evidence about Sheridan's texts so well marshalled by Mr Rhodes[2] again proves decisive. Sheridan had to adopt the same defence as Shakespeare and his Company of withholding his work from publication; and the same methods of piracy were open to the needy actors of Elizabethan times as were practised on Sheridan. *The Duenna* was first produced at Covent Garden in November 1775, but the first authorized edition did not appear till nearly twenty years later. This precaution did not prevent unauthorized provincial performances, and early in

[1] Dr Greg finds that *Orlando* is largely reported matter but not a shorthand report.

[2] *Sheridan*, ed. R. Crompton Rhodes: I, 255–268; II, 162–164.

1777 the piece was running both at the Royal and New Theatres in Dublin. The law courts refused Sheridan redress. A version of the opera described as that performed at the Theatre Royal Dublin was published. The precedent for these liberties was found in England: before the opera reached Dublin similar performances had already taken place in York and other centres, and Tate Wilkinson, manager of the Theatre Royal at York, has left on record how he made the version produced at his theatre.

> I locked myself in my room; set down first all the jokes I remembered, then I laid a book of the songs before me; and with magazines kept the regulation of the scenes; and by the help of a numerous collection of obsolete Spanish plays, I produced an excellent comic Opera.

This is the method of construction that, in the judgment of Mr Rhodes, the peculiarities of the edition of 1777 suggest. In spite, however, of Tate Wilkinson's approval of his own work, Mr Rhodes does not hesitate to call it an illiterate paraphrase.

This method was of course as practicable in Shakespeare's day as in Sheridan's, and there is actually an instance of this kind of report among the Bad Quartos. The compiler of *The Taming of a Shrew* anticipated Tate Wilkinson's device. He included in his compilation as many of the jokes from Shakespeare's *Taming of the Shrew* as he could remember, and filled out the piece with quotations from Marlowe. These latter interpolations have generally been recognized as borrowings, but perversely enough some still regard the other matter as the product of the compiler's original wit, to which Shakespeare is indebted. Samuel Hickson, however, as long ago as

1850, showed conclusively, if ever textual evidence was conclusively, that the pirate had given himself away here too by reproducing in some instances everything of Shakespeare's quip except the point.

As one might expect, and as the evidence proves, this was not the only method open to pirates. The history of *The School for Scandal* provides an example of what may be considered a more usual procedure. After the success of the comedy in London in 1777 several provincial performances were authorized. The manager of the theatre at Exeter was anxious to obtain a copy of the text; and being unable to procure a proper version he made use of one furnished him by an actor. John Bernard, the actor, has himself recorded his method.

Hughes, the manager, wanted a powerful novelty, and proposed *The School for Scandal*, then new and greatly discussed. Its success at Bath had dispersed its fame about the West of England, and it was highly probable that, if the play were produced at Exeter, it would run a number of nights to full houses. But the Comedy was not yet published and the managers who had copies of it, had obtained them on condition that they did not permit the same to become the parents of others. . . . Under these circumstances I offered to attempt a compilation of the comedy, if Mr Hughes would give me his word that the manuscript should be destroyed at the end of the season. This was agreed to, and I set about my task in the following manner. I had played Sir Benjamin at Bath and Charles at Richmond, and went on for Sir Peter one or two evenings when Edwin was indisposed; thus I had three parts in my possession. Dimond and Blissit (Joseph and Sir Oliver) transmitted theirs by post, on conveying the assurance to them which Mr Hughes had to me. Old Rowley was in the Company, and my wife had played both Lady Teazle and Mrs

Candour. With these materials for a groundwork, my general knowledge of the play collected in rehearsing and performing in it above forty times, enabled me in a week to construct a comedy in five acts, called, in imitation of the original, *The School for Scandal.*

Result, the public not being let into the secret the play drew crowded houses twice a week to the end of the season.

The peculiarities of *The Contention* and *Richard Duke of York* which have now to be considered in detail point to the employment of a similar method. The material composing them was supplied by actors who had played in 2 and 3 *Henry VI.* That a piracy could originate in this way is an obvious possibility. What is required to make it probable is an event that should affect the company possessing these plays so as to make the piracy profitable to some of its members. The history of Pembroke's men, to whom these plays may safely be attributed on the authority of the title page of *Richard Duke of York*, furnishes just such an accident. The plague kept them from acting in London during part of 1592 and 1593, but they were not able to make their expenses in the provinces. They had to return to London about the middle of August, and their financial condition was serious. This information was conveyed in a letter by Henslowe to Alleyn, who was himself in the provinces with Lord Strange's Company. It was written on 28 September 1593, and the relevant sentence runs:

As for my Lord of Pembroke's, which you desire to know where they be, they are all at home, and have been these five or six weeks, for they cannot save their charges with travel, as I hear, and were fain to pawn their apparel.

That the Company were now forced to part with

some of their more valuable books is practically
certain, for the following June when Lord Strange's
Company, now the Lord Chamberlain's men, returned to town, they began by performing plays which
had been in the possession of Pembroke's men.
Henslowe's diary only records the performance of
four pieces by the Chamberlain's men after the
plague, but three of these were plays of which his
complete record of their lengthy season immediately
before their tour makes no mention; they had
acquired them therefore after their departure, and
since two of them, *a Shrew* and *Titus Andronicus*, are
ascribed on early title pages to Pembroke's men, the
inference that the Chamberlain's men had purchased them from that company is natural.

With Pembroke's men forced to part with some
of their more valuable books to raise money, the
various methods of collaboration or individual effort
that were possible to the hard-pressed players, anxious
to put together versions to take again to the provinces,
are endless. And the very different conditions in
which some of their plays reached print reflect the
variety of possibilities. *Titus Andronicus* was published in 1594 in a good version; *The Taming of a
Shrew* in 1594 in a form as bad as *Titus* is good; *The
Contention* which also appeared in 1594, and *Richard
Duke of York* in 1595, occupy intermediate positions,
with the latter very much the better of the two texts.
It is impossible therefore to say without examination
how a Bad Quarto must have been constructed: the
two Sheridan piracies were of different kinds, and the
Shakespeare piracies, being more numerous, may offer
much greater variety in method. It is certain, for
example, that the conditions under which the later

plays were pirated were different from those that account for the Bad Quartos of 1594; it is even possible that in certain instances shorthand reporting may be part of the means to be considered; it is clear, however, that to insist that this alone can be the explanation of Bad Quartos is to take too much for granted, and is indeed to misrepresent or ignore the internal evidence.

(ii) *The Contention*

The scene from *The Contention* in which York advances his claim to the crown could easily have been written down from memory by someone who had witnessed the play, or by an actor who had once taken part in the scene. If its confusions are now to be attributed to the defective memory of an actor, what, it may be asked, is the objection to supposing that his memory or that of his fellows was equally defective when the shorthand reporter was present at their performances? It will be admitted, however, that an actor fresh from rehearsal, with his part in his pocket for consulting if necessary between the scenes, and with the prompter in close attendance, is in a very different position from the same individual deprived of his part, with no prompt book from which he can seek assistance, and owing to the misfortunes of his company unrehearsed in the piece for some weeks or months. Lack of practice and the lapse of time must both have affected his memory, and, in the absence of the necessary material with which it might be refreshed, he would naturally give a more imperfect report of his part than he was accustomed to do in the theatre; much would be remembered inexactly, and frequent confusions would not be surprising. This would be natural even when he attempted to remember the part he himself played, but if, in addition, he was also asked to reconstruct the parts of some of those with whom he played his difficulties would be greatly increased. These are the difficulties revealed in the blundering that marks York's part in the scene quoted from *The Contention*. It is too bad for bad report, if report be limited for the moment to shorthand reporting; it is not even good enough to be regarded as what could be remembered by the actor who played the part, when placed at the disadvantage already described; it is only what a fellow-actor in similar difficulties could remember of his words.

Warwick's part is also a report, but it does not stumble over the historical relationships, and is much nearer the Folio in sense and phrasing than that given to York. Since there is no need to insist that Warwick's part is given in the Quarto almost as it was delivered by the actor on the stage, it is possible to adopt the more obvious explanation, that this scene is a report by an actor who wrote down what he could remember of it. There would be no difficulty in accounting for the superiority of Warwick's part, if the actor who played in that rôle had a hand in constructing the report; he cannot at this point have had any manuscript of his part to refer to as he reproduced it from memory; but though his report is imperfect, he stumbles less when he is reproducing what he once declaimed himself than when he is trying to remember what other actors had to say.

The Quarto considered as a whole supports this explanation: Warwick's part all through is outstanding for its accuracy. In the last two scenes, for example, which contain in the Quarto about 100 lines, there are 20 lines which are very similar to the corresponding parts in the Folio, the rest is rubbish; of these 20 good lines 16 are spoken by Warwick, and 13 of them are given almost verbatim; Warwick's part for these two scenes extends in the Folio to 17 lines. The completeness of the part, which is combined in this scene with accuracy, is also characteristic of it as a whole: according to Malone's marking, Warwick is only given 10 lines in the Folio which are not found in some form or other in the Quarto; the addition is less than 10 per cent., whereas the Queen's part is increased by more than 120 per cent., York's by more than 60 per cent., and the King's by about 70 per cent.; and what the Quarto does reproduce of their parts is on the whole a very inferior report.

The only other part of which we have a reasonable account is Suffolk's. The actor playing in this is throughout opposed to Warwick, for although Suffolk is killed half-way through the story he lives again in Clifford, the same actor playing both parts. The Quarto text is very largely due to the amicable collaboration of these opposites. The following extract from *The Contention*, when compared with 2 *Henry VI*, Act III, sc. ii, l. 300, affords an example of his reporting, and shows how superior the version of his own lines is to that which he can supply of the Queen's.

The Contention (1594)

Queene. Hell fire and vengeance go along with you,
Theres two of you, the diuell make the third.

Fie womanish man, canst thou not curse thine enemies?
  Suffolke. A plague vpon them, wherefore should I curse them?
Could curses kill as do the Mandrakes groanes,
I would inuent as many bitter termes

Deliuered strongly through my fixed teeth,
With twise so many signes of deadly hate,
As leaue fast enuy in her loathsome caue,
My toong should stumble in mine earnest words,
Mine eyes should sparkle like the beaten flint,
My haire be fixt on end, as one distraught,
And euery ioynt should seeme to curse and ban,
And now me-thinks my burthened hart would breake,
Should I not curse them. Poison be their drinke,
Gall worse then gall, the daintiest thing they taste.
Their sweetest shade a groue of sypris trees.

Their softest tuch as smart as lyzards stings.
Their musicke frightfull, like the serpents hys.
And boding scrike-oules make the consort full.
All the foule terrors in darke seated hell.
  Queene. Inough sweete Suffolke, thou torments thy selfe.

  Suffolke. You bad me ban, and will you bid me sease?
Now by this ground that I am banisht from,
Well could I curse away a winters night,
And standing naked on a mountaine top,
Where byting cold would neuer let grasse grow,
And thinke it but a minute spent in sport.

The second Part of Henry the Sixt (1623)

Qu. Mischance and Sorrow goe along with you,
Hearts Discontent, and sowre Affliction,
Be play-fellowes to keepe you companie:
There's two of you, the Deuill make a third,
And three-fold Vengeance tend vpon your steps.
   Suff. Cease, gentle Queene, these Execrations,
And let thy *Suffolke* take his heauie leaue.
   Queen. Fye Coward woman, and soft harted wretch,
Hast thou not spirit to curse thine enemy.
   Suf. A plague vpon them: wherefore should I cursse
             them?
Would curses kill, as doth the Mandrakes grone,
I would inuent as bitter searching termes,
As curst, as harsh, and horrible to heare,
Deliuer'd strongly through my fixed teeth,
With full as many signes of deadly hate,
As leane-fac'd enuy in her loathsome caue.
My tongue should stumble in mine earnest words,
Mine eyes should sparkle like the beaten Flint,
Mine haire be fixt an end, as one distract:
I, euery ioynt should seeme to curse and ban,
And euen now my burthen'd heart would breake
Should I not curse them. Poyson be their drinke.
Gall, worse then gall, the daintiest that they taste:
Their sweetest shade, a groue of Cypresse Trees:
Their cheefest Prospect, murd'ring Basiliskes:
Their softest Touch, as smart as Lyzards stings:
Their Musicke, frightfull as the Serpents hisse,
And boading Screech-Owles, make the Consort full.
All the foule terrors in darke seated hell——
   Q. Enough sweet Suffolke, thou torment'st thy selfe,
And these dread curses like the Sunne 'gainst glasse,
Or like an ouer-charged Gun, recoile,
And turnes the force of them vpon thy selfe.
   Suf. You bad me ban, and will you bid me leaue?
Now by the ground that I am banish'd from,
Well could I curse away a Winters night,
Though standing naked on a Mountaine top,
Where byting cold would neuer let grasse grow,
And thinke it but a minute spent in sport.

Queene. No more. Sweete Suffolke hie thee hence to *France*,
Or liue where thou wilt within this worldes globe,
Ile haue an Irish that shall finde thee out,
And long thou shalt not staie, but ile haue thee repelde,
Or venture to be banished my selfe.
Oh let this kisse be printed in thy hand,
That when thou seest it, thou maist thinke on me.
Away, I say, that I may feele my griefe,
For it is nothing whilst thou standest here.

Suffolke. Thus is poore *Suffolke* ten times banished,
Once by the King, but three times thrise by thee

Enter *Vawse.*

Queene. How now, whither goes Vawse so fast?
Vawse. To signifie unto his Maiestie,
That Cardinall Bewford is at point of death,
Sometimes he raues and cries as he were madde,
Sometimes he cals upon Duke Humphries Ghost,
And whispers to his pillow as to him,
And sometime he calles to speake unto the King,

Qu. Oh, let me intreat thee cease, giue me thy hand,
That I may dew it with my mournfull teares:
Nor let the raine of heauen wet this place,
To wash away my wofull Monuments.
Oh, could this kisse be printed in thy hand,
That thou might'st thinke vpon these by the Seale,
Through whom a thousand sighes are breath'd for thee.
So get thee gone, that I may know my greefe,
'Tis but surmiz'd, whiles thou art standing by,
As one that surfets, thinking on a want:
I will repeale thee, or be well assur'd,
Aduenrure to be banished my selfe:
And banished I am, if but from thee.
Go, speake not to me; euen now be gone.
Oh go not yet. Euen thus, two Friends condemn'd,
Embrace, and kisse, and take ten thousand leaues,
Loather a hundred times to part then dye;
Yet now farewell, and farewell Life with thee.
Suf. Thus is poore Suffolke ten times banished,
Once by the King, and three times thrice by thee.
'Tis not the Land I care for, wer't thou thence,
A Wildernesse is populous enough,
So Suffolke had thy heauenly company:
For where thou art, there is the World it selfe,
With euery seuerall pleasure in the World:
And where thou art not, Desolation.
I can no more: Liue thou to ioy thy life;
My selfe no ioy in nought, but that thou liu'st.

Enter Vaux.

Queene. Whether goes *Vaux* so fast? What newes I
          prethee?
Vaux. To signifie vnto his Maiesty,
That Cardinall *Beauford* is at point of death:
For sodainly a greeuous sicknesse tooke him,
That makes him gaspe, and stare, and catch the aire,
Blaspheming God, and cursing men on earth.
Sometime he talkes, as if Duke *Humfries* Ghost
Were by his side: Sometime, he calles the King,
And whispers to his pillow, as to him,
The secrets of his ouer-charged soule,

And I am going to certifie vnto his grace,
That euen now he cald aloude for him.
  Queene. Go then good Vawse and certifie the King.
Exet Vawse.

Oh what is worldly pompe, all men must die,
And woe am I for Bewfords heauie ende.
But why mourne I for him, whilst thou art here?
Sweete Suffolke hie thee hence to France,
For if the King do come, thou sure must die.

  Suff. And if I go I cannot liue: but here to die,
What were it else, but like a pleasant slumber
In thy lap?
Here could I, could I, breath my soule into the aire,
As milde and gentle as the new borne babe,
That dies with mothers dugge betweene his lips,
Where from thy sight I should be raging madde,
And call for thee to close mine eyes,
Or with thy lips to stop my dying soule,
That I might breathe it so into thy bodie,
And then it liu'd in sweete Elyziam,
By thee to die, were but to die in ieast,
From thee to die, were torment more then death,
O let me staie, befall, what may befall.
  Queen. Oh mightst thou staie with safetie of thy life,
Then shouldst thou staie, but heauens deny it,
And therefore go, but hope ere long to be repelde.

  Suff. I goe.
  Queene. And take my heart with thee.
        She kisseth him.
  Suff. A iewell lockt into the wofulst caske,
That euer yet containde a thing of woorth,
Thus like a splitted barke so sunder we.
This way fall I to death.   *Exet Suffolke.*
  Queene. This way for me.   *Exet Queene.*

And I am sent to tell his Maiestie,
That euen now he cries alowd for him.
   Qu. Go tell this heauy Message to the King.   *Exit*
Aye me! What is this World? What newes are these?
But wherefore greeue I at an houres poore losse,
Omitting Suffolkes exile, my soules Treasure?
Why onely Suffolke mourne I not for thee?
And with the Southerne clouds, contend in teares?
Theirs for the earths encrease, mine for my sorrowes.
Now get thee hence, the King thou know'st is comming,
If thou be found by me, thou art but dead.
   Suf. If I depart from thee, I cannot liue,
And in thy sight to dye, what were it else,
But like a pleasant slumber in thy lap?
Heere could I breath my soule into the ayre,
As milde and gentle as the Cradle-babe,
Dying with mothers dugge betweene it's lips.
Where from thy sight, I should be raging mad,
And cry out for thee to close up mine eyes:
To haue thee with thy lippes to stop my mouth:
So should'st thou eyther turne my flying soule,
Or I should breathe it so into thy body,
And then it liu'd in sweete Elizium.
To dye by thee, were but to dye in iest,
From thee to dye, were torture more then death:
Oh let me stay, befall what may befall.
   Queen. Away: Though parting be a fretfull corosiue,
Ir is applyed to a deathfull wound.
To France sweet Suffolke: Let me heare from thee:
For wheresoere thou art in this worlds Globe,
Ile haue an *Iris* that shall finde thee out.
   Suf. I go.
   Qu. And take my heart with thee.
   Suf. A Iewell lockt into the wofulst Caske,
That euer did containe a thing of worth,
Euen as a splitted Barke, so sunder we:
This way fall I to death.
   Qu. This way for me.   *Exeunt*

This is a favourable example of the work of Warwick's collaborator, but he does not always reach this level of accuracy. Warwick himself is far more consistent, but allowance must be made for the heavier part Suffolk has to carry. This may explain why once or twice he fails badly, notably in Act iv, sc. viii; he never, however, has any difficulty in those scenes where he encounters Warwick, and returns his abuse and defiance. Act iii, sc. ii, where Suffolk and Warwick quarrel over the dead body of Duke Humphrey in the presence of the King, and Act v, sc. i, where Clifford and Warwick defy each other before the final engagement, show how their memories are quickened with the heat of their rhetorical exchanges, and how admirable a report of these encounters they can supply. Suffolk's farewell to Queen Margaret follows on one of their stormy passages, and Suffolk thoroughly roused is able to sustain his part, as one passion passes into another, through the change of mood to the very close of the scene.

But the copy for the Quarto does not everywhere consist of reported matter; it is occasionally based on transcription. From Act iv, sc. v the Folio reads:

Enter Lord Scales upon the Tower walking. Then enters two or three Citizens below.

Scales. How now? Is *Iacke Cade* slaine?
1. *Cit.* No my Lord, nor likely to be slaine:
    For they haue wonne the Bridge,
    Killing all those that withstand them:
    The L. Maior craues ayd of your Honor from the
      Tower
    To defend the City from the Rebels.
Scales. Such ayd as I can spare you shall command,
    But I am troubled heere with them my selfe,

The Rebels haue assay'd to win the Tower.
But get you to Smithfield, and gather head,
And thither I will send you *Mathew Goffe.*
Fight for your King, your Countrey, and your
Liues,
And so farwell, for I must hence againe. *Exeunt*

*Enter Iacke Cade and the rest, and strikes his
staffe on London stone.*

Cade. Now is *Mortimer* Lord of this City,

With this the Quarto closely corresponds:

Enter the Lord *Skayles* upon the Tower
walles walking.

Enter three or foure Citizens below.

Lord Scayles. How now, is Iacke Cade slaine?
1. *Citizen.* No my Lord, nor likely to be slaine,
For they haue wonne the bridge,
Killing all those that withstand them.
The Lord Mayor craueth ayde of your
honor from the Tower,
To defend the Citie from the Rebels.
Lord Scayles. Such aide as I can spare, you shall command,
But I am troubled here with them my selfe,
The Rebels haue attempted to win the
Tower,
But get you to Smythfield and gather head,
And thither I will send you Mathew Goffe,
Fight for your King, your Country, and your
liues,
And so farewell, for I must hence againe.
Exet omnes.

Enter *Iacke Cade* and the rest, and strikes his sword
upon London stone.

Cade. Now is Mortemer Lord of this Citie,

Since the first citizen speaks in prose the only explanation why both Quarto and Folio begin each line with the same word and initial capital is that they are derived from closely related manuscripts—unless it can be shown that the printers of the Folio used a Quarto edition for reference when setting up their version of 2 *Henry VI*. The compilers of the Quarto had here a manuscript at their disposal, and it cannot have consisted merely of actors' parts: the stage directions also correspond; and this is found elsewhere. At Act II, sc. iii, the Quarto directs:

> Enter at one doore the Armourer and his neighbours, drinking to him so much that he is drunken, and he enters with a drum before him, and his staffe with a sand-bag fastened to it, and at the other doore, his man with a drum and sand-bagge, and Prentises drinking to him.

The Folio gives the same directions:

> *Enter at one Doore the Armorer and his Neighbors, drinking to him so much, that hee is drunke; and he enters with a Drumme before him, and his Staffe, with a Sand-bagge fastened to it: and at the other Doore his Man, with a Drumme and Sand-bagge, and Prentices drinking to him.*

The dialogue that follows this direction is given in the Folio and Quarto almost word for word; each version has a few phrases not found in the other, but the Quarto is again clearly from a manuscript; and as before the manuscript available did not contain merely the scene itself, it also included the opening stage direction for the following scene:

> Enter Duke *Humphrey* and his men, in
> mourning cloakes.

This direction is also given in the Folio, the only

change being that the spelling of *Humphrey* is altered
to *Humfrey*. The carry over of the manuscript
material from one scene into the next is seen even
more clearly in the passage previously quoted; though
the scene changed from the Tower to London stone,
the manuscript was still available, but after supplying
more dialogue and another stage direction of some
length suddenly broke off with the words,

> thou shalt haue it
> For that word.

Both these passages of manuscript material begin
with the opening of a scene and end abruptly some-
where in the next scene: in Act II, sc. i we find in
the very middle of the scene the sudden appearance
of transcription with the words,

> And yet I thinke Ieat did he neuer see.

and this continues to the end of the episode, although
not of the scene, and concludes with the stage direction,

> After the Beadle hath hit him one girke, he leapes ouer
> the stoole and runnes away, and they run after him,
> crying, A miracle, a miracle.

The Folio stage direction is similar:

> *After the Beadle hath hit him once, he leapes ouer
> the Stoole, and runnes away: and they
> follow, and cry, A Miracle.*

There is no reason whatever to suppose that these
stage directions had their origin in the report put
together by the actors, or that they were incor-
porated in the Folio only because Jaggard's printers
took them from his 1619 reprint of the Quarto:

similar fool-proof instructions are found in the Folio in places where there can be no debt to the Quarto. In Act 1, sc. iv, although Bullingbrooke instructs Southwell to read, the stage direction provides an alternative, should the actor available for Southwell be unable to read Latin.

> *Here doe the Ceremonies belonging, and make the Circle,*
> *Bullingbrooke or Southwell reades,* Coniuro
> te, *&c. It Thunders and Lightens*
> *terribly: then the Spirit*
> *riseth.*

The Good Quarto of *Titus Andronicus* also shows that this kind of direction was found in good theatrical manuscripts. There can be no doubt therefore that here again, in the Quarto, dialogue and stage directions were taken from some manuscript.

The sudden appearance and equally sudden cessation of transcription of this kind in the course of the Quarto text can only be explained on the hypothesis that the compilers had at their disposal not only what they could remember of their own parts but a fragmentary transcript of the play. Some support for this suggestion is found in the lengths of the three passages so far referred to. The passage in which Duke Humphrey exposes the impostor at St Albans beginning in the Quarto at "And yet I thinke Ieat did he neuer see", and extending to the stage direction concluding "a miracle", occupies, when stage directions are counted (*exit* being omitted), 40 Quarto lines. The encounter between the Armourer and his man taken with the opening stage direction of the next scene requires 46 lines in the Quarto, and the passage beginning "Enter the Lord *Skayles*" and ending "For that word" has 42 lines. These passages may represent three pages preserved from a transcript.

In addition to these pages there are smaller fragments which have become detached in some way from the original mass and been embedded in the Quarto. The most considerable of these is York's speech at the close of Act i, sc. i, beginning, "*Anioy and Maine*, both giuen unto the French". In the same scene the articles of peace which Suffolk presents to the King are also transcribed material. They would be written on a piece of paper which could be read from on the stage. This paper might easily be preserved when much else was lost. It is strange, however, that the passage immediately following on the articles of peace, the investiture of Suffolk and the King's address, is also from a transcript. There is not enough, however, even with the terms of peace to permit us to assume that another page was available here; further, the dialogue between the articles is clearly only a report. The terms of peace were probably preserved by themselves.

This is almost certainly true of the questions put to the spirit in Act i, sc. iv, and the doubtful answers. These are found twice in both Folio and Quarto; the first time they occur as question and answer between Bullingbrooke and the spirit, the second time they are read from a scroll which York seizes when he breaks in on the so-called conspirators. In the Quarto they are embedded in the poorest of reported matter; the excuse, for example, which the spirit makes for its departure, "for I must hence again", is really that offered by Lord Scales to the citizens. The questions and answers, however, are given exactly as they stand in the Folio, with the exception of an unimportant inversion in the first line, and of the readings "fate away" for "fates await" and "betide" for "befall". When the scroll is read in the Folio it too has "betide" instead of "befall", and this suggests that the whole of this piece of matter in the Quarto, as well as this particular reading, came from the scroll. The Quarto compilers when they came to repeat the prophecies, possibly owing to their anxiety to interpolate suitable dialogue as in the Folio, transcribed them more loosely than they did when copying down their material directly and completely, as on the first occasion. The phrase, however, "fate awaits", which differs from the earlier readings in Quarto and Folio, agrees with what is read from the Folio scroll. The position of the direction *Reads* before the first answer in the Quarto, and its similar position in the Folio, together with the Folio omission of the first question, also suggest that some manuscript peculiarity explains both irregularities. It is unnecessary, however, to enter on conjecture as the evidence is sufficient to make it probable that the Quarto compilers had for this passage a detached scroll.

There remain three small pieces of transcription. The Armourer's part in Act I, sc. iii, the five lines given to Duke Humphrey in Act II, sc. iv, beginning, "Sweete Nell, ill can thy noble minde abrooke", and the least considerable in size of them all, the isolated stage direction in Act II, sc. i,

Enter the Maior of Saint Albones and his brethren with
Musicke, bearing the man that had bene blind,
betweene two in a chaire.

The corresponding Folio direction has been cut down a little, but preserves sufficient to show that the

Quarto gives a manuscript version. It is fortunately unnecessary for the present purpose to conjecture how exactly every part in *The Contention* came to be preserved. Enough has been established to show that in the construction of this text from fragments so minutely broken, and so fortuitously re-united, chances would operate which cannot now be calculated with completeness.

The evidence for the use of theatrical documents in the compilation of the Quarto confirms the conclusion deduced from the reported matter itself; taken together they prove that it could only have been actors who put together *The Contention*, actors who had been members of Pembroke's Company, and who had played in 2 *Henry VI*.

(iii) *Richard Duke of York*

Richard Duke of York is a compilation of a similar kind, but it differs from its twin piracy in detail. Although a fuller and more satisfactory version than *The Contention*, it contains none of the lengthy transcribed stage directions found there. The stage directions of 3 *Henry VI* are very similar to those of 2 *Henry VI*, but they have not found their way into the Quarto. If the actors had now any written material to assist their memories it was players' parts; but if their means differ in detail the chief agents in the piracy are the same. The impress of Warwick or Clifford can again be distinguished amid the confusion whenever either makes his entry.

Starting from the scene (Act IV, sc. i) between Edward and his brothers (part of which has already been examined in detail), where neither Warwick nor

Clifford is present, one can contrast it with the scene on each side where Warwick takes a leading part. Act III, sc. iii begins badly in the Quarto; at least six actors are on the stage, but the 40 lines or more of dialogue which precede the entry of Warwick are compressed into 10 lines that incorporate hardly a dozen words of the original. With the appearance of Warwick all is changed; so far the Quarto has dropped 35 out of the first 45 lines, but from now to the end of the scene, another 219 lines in the Folio, it only omits 60, and it gives not merely a much fuller version, it is on an entirely different level of accuracy. Warwick's own speeches are almost complete, and so accurate as to suggest that they were transcribed from a part in possession of the reporter. Such a part would contain not only Warwick's own lines but the concluding words of the speeches which he had to follow: this is what is found in the part of Orlando recently examined so carefully by Dr Greg, where the cue may consist of one, two or sometimes three words from the end of the last line in the preceding speech. In the scene before us, not only are Warwick's lines nearly complete, but the cue words are with two exceptions also included, and sometimes in speeches that are so reduced in reporting that the preservation of the final word is probably due to its presence in Warwick's part. When compared with what is found in Sheridan piracies Warwick's lines cannot be regarded as below the standard found in work probably transcribed from old theatrical parts.

The report of Act IV, sc. i, or Act III, sc. ii, the other interview between the new King and his brothers, is on a lower level. Act III, sc. i is even poorer stuff, and only at Act II, sc. vi, where War-

wick again plays a leading part, does the quality of the
text improve. Here Clifford also appears, and opens
the scene with his speech, "Here burns my candel
out". His importance may be quickly estimated by
turning back towards the beginning through Act ii,
sc. v, where, although the King, Queen, Prince and
Exeter, are present, there is hardly a good line, to
Act ii, sc. iv, where Clifford's presence is marked by
another very accurate speech from manuscript.

The poor matter which fills the gap between
Clifford's speeches illustrates two kinds of error that
are frequent in the reports.

Throughout the Quartos passages from different
scenes and even from the different parts of the whole
contention are confused in the reporter's memory.
When Suffolk in *The Contention*, Act iii, sc. i, l. 117,
says,

> And so thinke I Madame, for as you know,
> If our King Henry had shooke hands with death,

he is taking the second line from 3 *Henry VI*, Act i,
sc. iv, l. 102; similarly in *Richard Duke of York*, Act
ii, sc. vi, l. 94, Edward's line,

> We here create the Duke of *Clarence*, and girt thee with
> the sword.

incorporates the King's words to Suffolk in 2 *Henry
VI*, Act i, sc. i, l. 65. These *anticipations and recollections*, as Dr Greg has named them, are well illustrated in small compass in Act ii, sc. v. As the King
is lamenting his fortunes there enters a son that has
killed his father; when he realizes what he has done
he exclaims,

> Oh heauy times! begetting such Euents.

He is followed by a father who has killed his son and
who says,   Is this our Foe-mans face?
Ah, no, no, no, it is mine onely Sonne.

O pitty God, this miserable Age!
What Str[at]agems? how fell? how Butcherly?
Erreoneous, mutinous, and unnaturall,
This deadly quarrell daily doth beget?

The memory of the Quarto reporter, prompted by
the repetition of "beget", combined them.

But staie, me thinkes this is no famous face:
Oh no it is my sonne that I haue slaine in fight,
O monstrous times begetting such euents,
How cruel bloudy, and ironious,
This deadly quarrell dailie doth beget.

No doubt an actor, even when delivering his part
on the stage, has a tendency to similar mistakes, but
circumstances and the assistance available save him
from such gross errors as are everywhere found in
the Quartos. This blunder indeed points to someone
who had never studied the part in manuscript trying
to report it, and confusing it with a similar part; it is an
actor's attempt to reconstruct the lines spoken by one
of his fellows.

The other kind of error found in the scene is what
might be expected in these circumstances. The Folio
line,

Was euer sonne, so rew'd a Fathers death?

becomes,

Was euer son so rude his fathers bloud to spil?

and "famous face" for "foeman's face" is another
error of hearing. But it would be a mistake to suppose

that this class of error is peculiar to a stenographic report.[1] If Warwick was trying to reconstruct these parts from what he remembered of their delivery, he could make mistakes of hearing just as easily as a shorthand reporter, and more easily, for what he heard he had now to try to remember. These errors are quite characteristic of the method of reconstruction which is now being offered as an explanation, and an example can be seen in the passage quoted from *The Duenna* where *rustling* becomes *rattling*.

(iv) The interpolations from *Edward II*

Both the classes of error illustrated from Act II, sc. v have several varieties; here it is only necessary to examine one kind of *anticipation and recollection* in more detail. Not only may the actors transfer lines from scene to scene and part to part, they may borrow lines and expressions from other plays with which they are familiar. Such transferences are found in the later piracies from Shakespeare: the Bad Quarto of *Hamlet* incorporates in its text a line from *Twelfth Night*, and *The Merry Wives of Windsor* (1602) borrows a line from *Hamlet*. In *The Contention* and *Richard Duke of York* there are several passages which seem to be *recollections* of this kind. The lines about "the wilde Onele", which Malone offered as evidence that the Quartos were original drafts, are very similar to these in *Edward II*,

> The wilde *Oneyle*, with swarmes of Irish Kernes,
> Liues uncontroulde within the English pale.

---

[1] The problem is well treated in Dr Greg's "*Alcazar* and *Orlando*", p. 258.

Standing in a poorly reported scene they have all the marks of an interpolation by the actor or actors, and confirmation for this is found on the title page of *Edward II*, which marks it as another play in the repertory of Pembroke's Company. The transference of passages from *Edward II* would be very natural in the circumstances in which, it has been argued, certain of Pembroke's players put together *The Contention* and *Richard Duke of York*.

When Malone, giving up his earlier speculations about Greene and Peele, followed Farmer and assigned the Quartos to Marlowe, he did so because of the many similarities of expression between them and *Edward II*, that about "Onele" being one. This may very well be regarded as an insertion by the actors from *Edward II*, but Malone's claim cannot be put aside without further examination because it rests in part only on these insertions. There are in the Quartos parallels with *Edward II* which stand there because they were present in the work of the author of the original plays, being found in 2 and 3 *Henry VI*. In recent years this claim for Marlowe has been strengthened by Professor Tucker Brooke, who has made considerable additions to the list of parallels between 2 and 3 *Henry VI* and the plays of Marlowe, especially *Edward II* and *The Massacre at Paris*; in addition he recognizes, as Malone did not, that *The Contention* and *Richard Duke of York* are imperfect versions of the plays they profess to represent. He might well therefore admit the argument so far as it has determined the class of text to which the Quartos belong, and still deny the validity of the very important distinction that is now being made in his list of Marlowe parallels.

The parallel passages[1] may be divided into the following ten groups, each group connecting two plays:

(i) *The Contention* and *Edward II*: 5, 8, 11, 29, 30, 31.

(ii) *The Contention* and *Tamburlaine*: 7, 14.

(iii) *The Contention* and *Dido*: 1.

(iv) *The Contention* and *The Massacre at Paris*: 9.

There is nothing more to connect *Dido* and *The Contention* than the phrases "his eyes doe pearce" and "her speech doth pierce"; and the only parallel expressions noted in *The Massacre at Paris* and *The Contention* are "the panges of death doth gripe his heart" and "A griping paine hath ceasde upon my heart". These groups may therefore be ignored. The recollections from *Tamburlaine*, though few, are more convincing: the lines (*The Contention*, p. 17, ll. 14–16),

Night,
Wherein the Furies maske in hellish troupes,
Send up I charge you from *Sosetus* lake.

recall *Tamburlaine*, ll. 1999 and 3202,

Furies from the blacke *Cocitus* lake.
As is the Island where the Furies maske.

As *Tamburlaine* was a widely known play by 1594 there is nothing surprising in these interpolations. That the echoes from *Edward II* are *The Contention's* largest debt to Marlowe is also what the date and

[1] Professor Tucker Brooke has given his list in *The Transactions of the Connecticut Academy of Arts and Sciences*. Nos. 1–28 are given on pp. 164–9; those numbered above 32–6 are given on pp. 184–5; nos. 29–31 are additions to his list. The numbers after each group in the text indicate which of Professor Tucker Brooke's parallels fall within that group.

circumstances of its production would lead us to expect. The echoes naturally arise, as in the "Onele" passage, when some circumstance or phrase in 2 *Henry VI* reminds the pirate actor of something similar in *Edward II*. For example, the lines in 2 *Henry VI*, Act II, sc. iii,

> I see no reason, why a King of yeeres
> Should be to be protected like a Child.

and those in *Edward II*, ll. 1336–7,

> As though your highnes were a schoole boy still,
> And must be awde and gouernd like a child.

are similar in idea; the Quarto reporter confused them, and in the confusion his memory caught up another line,

> Did you regard the honor of your name,

which is closely connected with the *Edward II* passage, standing a few lines earlier in the same play. The result of this process is given in the Quarto (p. 12) as:

> And nere regards the honour of his name,
> But still must be protected like a childe,
> And gouerned by that ambitious Duke.

The reporter, however, has anticipated the passage in 2 *Henry VI* that started his memory on the combination, and sets down his new version four scenes earlier than the original passage. A similar confusion of phrase or situation accounts for the following parallels:

29. *The Contention*, p. 37,

> But haue you no greater proofes then these?

Edward II, l. 2611,

> But hath your grace no other proofe then this?

30. *The Contention*, p. 40,

And long thou shalt not staie, but ile haue thee repelde,

Edward II, ll. 410–11,

> And long thou shalt not stay, or if thou doost
> Ile come to thee.

31. *The Contention*, p. 9,

> But ere it be long, Ile go before them all,
> Despight of all that seeke to crosse me thus.

Edward II, ll. 897–8,

> Nay all of them conspire to crosse me thus
> But if I live, ile tread upon their heads.

The phrase in 2 *Henry VI* which suggested the lines in *Edward II* to the pirate, "smooth my way upon their headlesse neckes", has not found a place in the 1594 Quarto.

(v) 2 *Henry VI* and *Edward II*: 3, 6, 32, 33.

(vi) 2 *Henry VI* and *The Massacre at Paris*: 2, 4, 10, 13.

There are passages in 2 *Henry VI* that recall lines from Marlowe, but unlike those in the first group they have usually only a general resemblance in idea. The lines in 2 *Henry VI*, Act i, sc. iii, ll. 53–6,

> I tell thee *Poole*, when in the Citie *Tours*
> Thou ran'st a-tilt in honor of my Loue,
> And stol'st away the Ladies hearts of France;
> I thought King *Henry* had resembled thee.

remind us of those in *Edward II*, ll. 2516–18,

> Tell *Isabell* the Queene, I lookt not thus,
> When for her sake I ran at tilt in Fraunce
> And there unhorste the Duke of *Cleremont*.

but they are not like those in group (i), a re-arrange-
ment of similar phrases. There are only a few merely
phrasal parallels, e.g.

33. 2 *Henry VI*, Act I, sc. iii, l. 83,
    She beares a Dukes Reuenewes on her backe,
Edward II, l. 704,
    He wears a lords reuenwe on his back.

(vii) 3 *Henry VI* and *Edward II*: 15, 16, 18, 19,
23, 25, 26, 28, 35.
(viii) 3 *Henry VI* and *The Massacre at Paris*: 20,
21, 24.
(ix) 3 *Henry VI* and *The Jew of Malta*: 22, 36.
(x) 3 *Henry VI* and *Tamburlaine*: 12, 27, 34.

Unlike *The Contention, Richard Duke of York*
contains no noted parallel with Marlowe's work
which is not also found in its original 3 *Henry VI*.
This difference is explained by the better condition
of this text, and the fact that 3 *Henry VI* does not
present as does 2 *Henry VI* a number of situations
closely resembling those in *Edward II*. The phrases
common to 3 *Henry VI* and *Edward II* are usually
mere tags: *dying in bands, Jove's tree, The Cedar* and
the Eagle. The following resemblances, however, are
more notable:

16. 3 *Henry VI*, Act I, sc. i, l. 239,
    Sterne *Falconbridge* commands the Narrow Seas,
Edward II, l. 970,
    The hautie *Dane* commands the narrow seas.

28. 3 *Henry VI*, Act v, sc. vi, ll. 61–2,
What? will the aspiring blood of Lancaster
Sinke in the ground? I thought it would haue mounted.

Edward II, l. 93,

> Frownst thou thereat, aspiring Lancaster?

Edward II, ll. 1999–2000,

> highly scorning, that the lowly earth
> Should drinke his bloud, mounts up into the ayre:

35. *3 Henry VI,* Act ii, sc. iii, l. 56,

> Foreslow no longer, make we hence amaine.

Edward II, l. 1138,

> Foreslow no time, sweet Lancaster, lets march.

There is at least one very close parallel in group (viii).

20. *3 Henry VI,* Act ii, sc. i, ll. 68–9,

> Sweet Duke of Yorke our Prop to leane upon,
> Now thou art gone, wee haue no Staffe, no Stay.

The Massacre at Paris, l. 1122,

> Sweet Duke of *Guise* our prop to leane upon,
> Now thou art dead, heere is no stay for us.

There is nothing of importance in groups (ix) and (x).

The separation between groups (i) and (ii), which contain actors' borrowings from Marlowe, and groups (v)–(x), which give the author's parallels with Marlowe, depends on the conclusion that *The Contention* is only a Bad Quarto; but Professor Tucker Brooke cannot immediately be forced to accept this distinction between his parallels, for the relation of *The Contention* and *Richard Duke of York* to 2 and 3 *Henry VI* is, he insists, more complicated than that so far considered. Between 2 and 3 *Henry VI* and the Quartos he discovers two complete plays (say X and Y) by Marlowe, which are, he claims, the plays imperfectly represented in *The Contention* and

Richard Duke of York: X and Y did not become 2 and 3 *Henry VI* till Shakespeare had rehandled them, so they may well have included matter which found a place in the Quartos but which was excised at Shakespeare's revision. The absence from the Folio, therefore, of such a passage as that about the "wild Onele", and others in groups (i) and (ii), need not prevent Professor Tucker Brooke's arguing that they stood in the Marlowe originals he discovers for the Quartos.

The unknowns, X and Y, enable Professor Tucker Brooke to offer a solution to a further difficulty in the parallels with Marlowe. Since it is on these parallels he claims the Quartos and their originals for Marlowe, he is forced to make this distinction between X and Y and the new matter of the 1623 versions added by Shakespeare: the Marlowe parallels he insists are peculiar to the early originals, while Shakespeare's part in the Folio shows an entirely different manner. Professor Tucker Brooke actually finds some of the resemblances to *Edward II* (Nos. 32–6) in those parts of the text first printed in 1623, but his hypothetical X and Y permit him to argue that these passages stood in the Marlowe originals of 1594–5 without finding their way into the Quartos. Had the Quartos been good texts of X and Y, he would have found the additional parallels there beside the others.

The unknown plays by Marlowe contained, according to Professor Tucker Brooke, all the Marlowe parallels found in the Quartos or in the Folio; and they show further marks of Marlowe's hand. Marlowe, it is said, not only repeats himself from play to play but within the limits of the same play; and the Quartos are Professor Tucker Brooke's evidence that

this trick must have been carried to excess in X
and Y. He gives only fifteen examples of repetition
within the Quartos, but the list could easily be greatly
extended. In quoting, for example, the words of the
dying Warwick,

> For manie wounds receiu'd, and manie moe repaid,
> Hath robd my strong knit sinews of their strength,
> And spite of spites needes must I yeeld to death.

which repeat what he has already said in Act II, sc. iii,
Professor Tucker Brooke omits the other repetitions
that connect these two scenes. The words that follow,

> And saie, commend me to my valiant brother,
>
> . . . .
>
> And so the valiant *Montague* gaue up the ghost.

remind us of the earlier Quarto passage,

> *Richard,* commend me to my valiant sonne,
>
> . . . .
>
> And so the noble Salsbury gaue up the ghost.

Presumably this is another instance of Marlowe's
habit of repeating himself. The Quartos have, however, even more instructive instances. The last scene
but one of *The Contention* has this threefold repetition:

> 34 For now my heart hath sworne immortall hate
> To thee and all the house of Lancaster.
>
> . . . .
>
> 48   I sweare,
> Immortall hate unto the house of Yorke,
>
> . . . .
>
> 57 To whom my soule hath sworne immortall hate.

There follows the stage direction,

> Enter *Richard,* and then *Clifford* laies down his father,
> fights with him, and *Richard* flies away againe.

The preceding lines are presumably marked as
Marlowe's not merely by the repetition but by the
phrase "sinowes shrinke" at line 40, which recalls
the "sinews shake" of *Tamburlaine*. None of the
repetitions in this paragraph is found in 2 or 3
Henry VI; are we to suppose they come from the
original *X* and *Y* which Professor Tucker Brooke
has told us of?

If so something more is now known about the
Marlowe originals; but there is no doubt that the
more extensive this information the more perplexing
the questions it suggests; for these originals now appear
to contain all those repetitions which seemed at an
earlier stage in this inquiry examples of a corruption
characteristic of texts pirated by actors, and several
repetitions that Professor Tucker Brooke particularly
ascribes to Marlowe have been confidently cited as
actors' interpolations. It must be admitted that *X* and
Y would be very curious originals if they contained
all the repetitions found in the Quartos. No doubt
Professor Tucker Brooke admits that certain repetitions are due to actors: he has not, when emphasizing
the difference in the conception of the characters
between the versions, touched on the unusual picture
of Richard presented in the stage direction that
follows the thrice repeated "immortal hate". Presumably he accepts this page in the Quarto, without
parallel in the Folio, as the work of the pirate; but
this admission at once places him in a difficulty: how
does he distinguish between the repetitions of Marlowe and the repetitions of the actors, and how can
he decide whether an echo from *Edward II*, or *The
Massacre at Paris*, is original to the text, or an interpolation? That he should have some criterion is

clear; for how else is he entitled to insist that X and Y included those traces of Marlowe first printed in the Folio, while excluding the rest of the 1623 text his theory does not require? He cannot refer us to the Folio as in general the guide in making these distinctions, for it is at the most critical moment in the discussion that he puts aside its authority most decisively. His conclusion as to what belongs to the original of the 1594–5 texts, and what has been added in the Folio, is framed to suit his hypothesis that the earliest version of 2 and 3 *Henry VI* is Marlowe's. X and Y are assumptions to make this hypothesis work, but it is impossible to take on trust from Professor Tucker Brooke what was or was not in these versions, till he can first prove that the hypothesis that demands them is itself necessary.

To this it might be replied that Professor Tucker Brooke has assumed the existence of X and Y, because of the differences he discovers between much of the new matter in the 1623 text and what can reasonably be presumed from the Quartos to belong to their originals. These differences he has tried to establish (*a*) on metrical, (*b*) on what may be called literary grounds.

Metrical tests are difficult to apply in this instance, for the counting of double-endings and similar verse phenomena on which they depend cannot be very reliable when one of the texts is admittedly corrupt. Professor Tucker Brooke recognizes this difficulty, but proceeds to count good and bad lines indifferently and to tabulate the results; he should, however, establish his distinction between those parts of the Quartos that are recognized as giving a good version of X and Y and those parts of the Folio text he claims

as Shakespeare's additions. He has failed to make this
comparison between what is actually comparable;
and had he not given his attention to finding a common measure for what is incommensurable, he would
have seen that the proper application of his own tests
disproves his assertions. This may be illustrated from
what Professor Pollard has described as the most
crucial passage for the decision between Marlowe
and Shakespeare, the scene containing the line
quoted by Greene in his attack on Shakespeare. It
is fortunately preserved in the Quarto in a form very
nearly satisfactory, at least from the entry of the
Queen, Clifford and Northumberland, at line 15;
York's opening soliloquy is obviously badly reported
and contains interpolated matter. We may begin our
investigation therefore from l. 16 and count to l. 165,
which concludes the scene; this corresponds to ll. 27–
180 in the Folio, and is on the whole very well
reported, so well reported that we can see that the
1623 and 1595 texts must have coincided at this
place. A count therefore of these Folio lines cannot
misinterpret to any extent the style of verse that here
stood in the 1594–5 originals. If Professor Tucker
Brooke is correct in his estimate of the characteristics
of this early verse, we should find a low percentage
of double endings, not more than 5 per cent.; but in
the 154 lines before us there are 22 double endings
or about 14 per cent., which is the figure Professor
Tucker Brooke gives for what he regards as Shakespeare's additions in 3 *Henry VI*, as a whole. This
important passage does not therefore differ in this
particular characteristic from the new matter; and
even if it should be claimed that the Folio here may
not exactly represent the 1595 text and that Shake-

speare might have gone over the verse adding double
endings, he can only have added 4, for the Quarto
contains 18, which is 12 per cent., a much higher
figure than Professor Tucker Brooke finds in Marlowe. It may be noted in passing that Mr J. M.
Robertson would, in all probability, unlike Professor
Tucker Brooke, find the percentage of double
endings in the scene just examined proof of Marlowe's
hand. The basis on which these tests stand is still very
uncertain; this is, however, discussed on pages 149–
152 and need not delay the decision against Professor
Tucker Brooke: he has failed to establish the distinction between the 1594–5 texts and those of 1623
by the metrical tests he would himself recognize as
valid.

His literary evidence must be passed over even
more briefly. A different view from that maintained
by him about Shakespeare's plotting and characterization will be found in the concluding chapter, but
as no absolutely demonstrable assertions can be advanced on these matters they can only be considered
after all the more material evidence has been examined. It is sufficient at this point to observe that
Professor Tucker Brooke's arguments on the literary
evidence are often open to serious question. In
comparing the passages[1] that liken Queen Margaret's
fortunes to a ship and her supporters to the mast and
tackle, he finds that the Quarto lines are "natural",
while the Folio version seems to him in comparison
"immature". But surely the Quarto is only giving
a shamefully mangled report of the Folio lines, and in
its confusion has even anticipated an expression in the
following scene. Professor Tucker Brooke's literary

[1] 3 *Henry VI*, Act v, sc. iv.

distinctions therefore are too doubtful to be regarded as evidence at this stage of the inquiry.

(v) *The Whole Contention*

The hypothetical originals by Marlowe have not been found either satisfactory in themselves or required by the evidence, and Professor Tucker Brooke's interpretation of one important piece of textual fact reveals how their assumption leads to untenable conclusions. The reprint of the Quartos which Jaggard issued in 1619 under the title, *The Whole Contention betweene the two Famous Houses, Lancaster and Yorke*, is supposed by Professor Tucker Brooke to contain additions which point to some such originals as *X* and *Y* being in his possession: his reprint not only brings the text in some instances nearer that of the Folio, it also draws on an independent source, since it has historical matter which is neither in the Quartos nor the Folio.

The scene which exhibits the most numerous corrections in the 1619 edition is that already quoted in which York details his pedigree; the most glaring errors in the list of Edward's sons and their descendants are now corrected, although others less serious are introduced. The addition most important for the present question is the passage about the elder son of the Black Prince:

Now *Edward* the blacke Prince dyed before his Father, leauing behinde him two sonnes, *Edward* borne at *Angolesme*, who died young, and *Richard* that was after crowned King, by the name of *Richard* the second, who dyed without an heyre.

No information about the Prince's first son is found

either in the earlier Quartos or in the Folio; nor is
there any probability of its having stood in the Folio
text, where we are told that the Black Prince left
behind him "Richard his only son". How then did
it find its way into the 1619 text? For it contains
accurate historical information that must have come
from some reliable source. Was this the Marlovian
X? If it was, why did not the corrector at the same
time put right the other mistakes in the scene, and
add those passages so necessary to explain the connection between the third branch of the family and
the fifth? The original *X* cannot have been identical
in this scene with the 1619 reprint, but must have
been almost the same as the text of 1623. Professor
Tucker Brooke here takes refuge in vagueness and
says:

It is by no means to be supposed, I think, that all the
necessary corrections of the Millington (1594) text, or
even all the better readings accessible to Pavier in Manuscript, are embodied in the 1619 edition.

It is obvious that *all* the *necessary* corrections of
the 1594 text are *not* found in that of 1619; but why
if Pavier had *X* in a good text before him did he not
make the necessary corrections? Could he not print
from his good copy? Or are we to suppose he was so
lazy that he would not fill in the necessary corrections,
but contented himself with putting in a few at
random throughout the play, while the mass remained in its hopeless state of corruption. Professor
Tucker Brooke must make this assumption, or conclude that all he had at his disposal was another bad
version of *X*, not quite so corrupt perhaps as that
printed in 1594, but very nearly as bad; for the scene

under discussion is the only one where any serious effort has been made to improve the text. The multiplication of bad versions is not an attractive hypothesis, but it is inevitable on Professor Tucker Brooke's assumptions, for there can be no doubt that several of the corrections made in the edition of 1619 are as clearly reported matter as anything in the earlier text.

There are a few additions in the 1619 text in Act 1, sc. ii, but some of this additional matter is very imperfect. In the Folio we find Elianor's threat,

> I would remoue these tedious stumbling blockes,
> And smooth my way upon their headlesse neckes.

which is not reported in the 1594 text. In that of 1619 it stands,

> I'de reach to'th Crowne, or make some hop headlesse.

The line itself is unmetrical, and the other new matter in which it stands is equally without rhythm; it is reported, and the reporter, in trying to restore what stands in the 1623 version, partially anticipates a line two scenes later,

> Would make thee quickly hop without thy Head.[1]

Another of the changes introduced in 1619 is equally instructive. "*Margery Iordaine* the cunning Witch of *Ely*", is now described as "of *Rye*". In the Folio her domicile is not given, although she is called by Holinshed "the witch of Eie". The Folio line in Act 1, sc. ii must have originally read,

> With *Margery Jordane* the cunning witch of *Eie*.

---

[1] "I'le make him hoppe headlesse".
The Troublesome Reign of King John, Part 1, p. 33.

The phrase "of *Eie*" was dropped by mistake in printing or from unnecessary scruples about the metre, only not before it had left its trace in the two clear corruptions of 1594 and 1619. If Jaggard had another text to go on it is obvious it was only another bad one.

Before another bad version of X is created it is necessary to note that for none of the additions in the 1619 text that can be regarded as good matter, except one, would it have been necessary to go any further than to a performance of 2 or 3 *Henry VI*. Some of the faulty additions are only bad shots at what would have been heard there, and the few insertions, not from that source, like the lines quoted by Professor Tucker Brooke,

> For he is like him every kind of way

and

> Under pretence of outward seeming ill

are not so remarkable as to require any other explanation than the ingenuity or zeal of the reviser. The one addition that does require us to look for a source independent of the two versions printed in 1594–5 and 1623 is the phrase, "*Edward* borne at *Angolesme*". But we need not create two whole plays by Marlowe to find an independent source for this one phrase since it stands in Holinshed. The reviser of the 1619 edition, in his effort to put York's pedigree in order, consulted that Chronicler; he managed to get the easy part correct whether from Holinshed or the theatre; in his endeavours he inserted this extra piece of information from the Chronicles, but by tacking it on to an old phrase created a new error, for at the death of the Black

Prince only one of his sons was alive. Those errors, however, in the scene that would have required for their removal a more extensive and intelligent use of Holinshed he was content to leave alone, and he made no attempt to supply the additions so necessary to make York's case convincing or even intelligible.

That Jaggard had no manuscript at his disposal is a fair inference from the corrections he made; and the circumstances under which he reprinted the Quartos confirm this conclusion. *The Whole Contention* was not issued by itself in 1619, but as Professor Pollard and Dr Greg[1] have proved as part of a volume containing eight other plays attributed to Shakespeare. Some of these were not by Shakespeare, others were his but in stolen versions, while only three were reprinted from Good Quartos. Jaggard, however, seems to have taken some pains with this doubtful venture, though he must have known the mixed quality of his wares: he even had the good texts corrected in places. A few of these corrections undoubtedly brought the text nearer that of the original, but we are not entitled to conclude because of this that Jaggard had any manuscript of *A Midsummer Night's Dream* or *The Merchant of Venice*[2] to work from: the manner in which he produced his volume makes it clear he had not. To suppose he had a manuscript for *The Whole Contention* is to misinterpret the textual and to ignore the bibliographical evidence at our disposal.

[1] *Shakespeare Folios and Quartos*, p. 81.
[2] See *The Merchant of Venice* (Cambridge University Press, 1926), p. 176.

(vi) The True Originall Copies

The decisive answer, however, to Professor Tucker Brooke's hypothesis is found in a comparison of the Quartos of 1594–5 as a whole with the Folio version of 1623. Since there is less difference between *Richard Duke of York* and *3 Henry VI* than between the other pair their evidence is for the present purpose more explicit, and may be taken first.

In a compilation such as *Richard Duke of York* has proved to be, it is only to be expected that much of the original would be mangled in reporting and many passages omitted altogether; but matter first found in bulk in the Folio can often be established as part of the original the actors had in their minds from isolated scraps that have stuck in their memories. One example from another Bad Quarto will show how much can sometimes be inferred from a single line. *Henry V* (1600) omits the second scene in the French camp, but tacks on the last line found there in the Folio to an imperfect report of the first scene. This has made nonsense of the situation, for it introduces the sun from the second scene, that takes place at morning, into the first whose time is midnight. Dr Greg[1] has no hesitation in concluding that this single line establishes the presence of the missing scene in the original the reporter was working from. The application of similar considerations reduces the matter in *3 Henry VI* that cannot be accounted for to very small dimensions.

The Folio text of *3 Henry VI* contains about 2900 lines. Of these Malone has marked approxi-

---

[1] *Shakespeare's Merry Wives of Windsor*, edited by Dr W. W. Greg, p. xix.

mately 735 as not found in some form in the Quarto. This cannot be regarded as more than might be expected to be missing from such a compilation as the Quarto, and unless these 735 lines were very markedly different from the remainder of the play they could simply be regarded as omissions by the reporter. But Malone's figures for new matter are subject to very considerable deductions. We find for instance that two very similar scenes have been confused in the Quarto report: in Act iv, sc. vi Warwick restores Henry to the throne but is disturbed by the news that Edward has escaped to Burgundy; in sc. viii there is the further news that Edward has crossed from Belgia and landed in the North. In the Quarto this second scene is tacked on to a poor report of the first half of sc. vi; the news of Edward's escape is cut out, and his return announced straight away. The Folio sequence of scenes is much more probable, and it can be established that the disturbance is the result of confusion in the reporter's memory, from a scrap of the missing part of sc. vi turning up inopportunely elsewhere. In the Quarto report of Act iv, sc. iii, Clarence concludes the episode by saying:

> What followes now all hithertoo goes well,
> But we must dispatch some letters to *France*,
> To tell the *Queene* of our happy fortune,
> And bid her come with speed to ioine with us.

The phrase "all hithertoo goes well" is a recollection of the opening line of the scene before, while the latter portion anticipates one of Henry's missing speeches in sc. vi,

> That *Margaret* your Queene, and my Sonne *Edward*,
> Be sent for, to returne from France with speed.

Malone has starred these lines in the Folio as new matter, but the Quarto itself provides evidence of their presence in the original, and there can be little doubt that these scenes stood from the first as in the Folio. Malone's Folio additions were merely Quarto omissions.

Again, it is always in those scenes and parts where the Quarto lines are defective in sense and metre that the "additions" are most numerous.

The scene between Henry and the father who had killed his son and the son who had killed his father has already been singled out for its corrupt condition, and here Malone stars 62 lines as Folio additions. The short scene between the King and the Keepers (Act III, sc. i), equally marked in the Quarto by anticipations and recollections as poor report, has 56 new lines in the Folio. This high proportion of additions to bad parts is well illustrated in Act III, sc. iii: of the 43 lines, all between the Queen and Lewis, that precede Warwick's entry, Malone marks 39 as entirely new matter; of the 222 lines that follow the entry of the reporter-actor only 56 are starred, and of these 27 are lines given to the Queen, 14 to Lewis, while no more than 8 are in Warwick's part, which is the heaviest of them all. Once we recognize the actor who played Warwick as an agent in the production of the Quarto text, the difference in the "additions" to various parts is to be explained by the means at the disposal of the reporters, not by the artistic feelings of a reviser.

The Queen's part throughout the play is very badly given. The opening scene (273 lines) of the play has 40 starred lines in Malone's text, and 19 of these are in the Queen's part, which extends to no more than 41 lines; further, its relative insufficiency in the Quarto is even lower than these figures suggest. The same story is true throughout. We would have to suppose on Professor Tucker Brooke's theory that the Queen's part was very extensively revised by Shakespeare for the 1623 text. But this part in 3 *Henry VI* is homogeneous with the rest of the play: nothing in its style, tone or matter points it out as a later addition; everything marks it as part of the original conception. If the Quarto therefore is accepted as an actor's compilation it is impossible to accept what Malone has marked as additions to the Queen's part as anything but the omissions of the reporters.

Had the original text of 1595 been as different from that of 1623, as Professor Tucker Brooke has surmised, we should expect to find at least some good matter in the Quarto that clearly had no place in Shakespeare's revision. There are no such passages. The three lines in Act v, sc. i that centre on Edward's "Et tu Brute", and three lines of Richard's in Act iv, sc. i,

> For why hath Nature made me halt downe right,
> But that I should be valiant and stand to it,
> For if I would, I cannot runne awaie.

are not found in the Folio; but the first is a clear omission, being implied in the business of the scene, and the second instance does not justify a revision theory. Good texts have occasional lapses, and none of the patches where the Quarto text challenges that of the Folio is evidence of the revision Professor Tucker Brooke has in mind.

Richard Duke of York, in spite of its deficiencies,

gives a text too close to that of 3 *Henry VI* to permit of their separation by any third version; there is not only nothing in 3 *Henry VI* that can be proved to be matter added to the original from which the Quarto was taken, there is next to nothing in 3 *Henry VI* that the Quarto version does not entitle us to suppose was there when the piracy took place.

The gap between *The Contention* and 2 *Henry VI* being greater might seem to leave more room for conjecture; but once *Richard Duke of York* is admitted to come from 3 *Henry VI* it will hardly be maintained that *The Contention* is from any other original than 2 *Henry VI*. Even here an examination of the lines on which the Quarto is constructed establishes 2 *Henry VI* as the only original. Warwick and Suffolk (later Clifford) are the two actors on whose parts the text is built. Where these parts are unmistakably good they are the same as in the Folio, and only diverge from that text where corruption can easily be established. These actors had in addition some manuscript material; where this is transcribed the differences from the Folio are so trifling that there can be no question of a third and independent version. The more satisfactory the Quarto text, the more certain it appears that 2 *Henry VI* is the only source.

Professor Tucker Brooke's assumptions are of a kind that demand detailed examination; he has himself, however, put very briefly the reasons for his error. In correcting those who ascribe the Quartos to many hands he says:

It is largely on the basis of…textual impurity that the theory of double or triple authorship of our plays has arisen, the tendency being to ascribe to the poet what has survived more or less in its original state, while assigning to another whatever the theatrical manipulator and the printer's devil have united in deforming.

But his own division of 2 and 3 *Henry VI* into two is open to the same objection. He had not sufficiently examined the textual problem before he took up that of authorship, and having decided that Marlowe's hand is clearly seen in the plays, he gratuitously adds the name of Shakespeare, no doubt as a concession to Heminge and Condell: they published the plays as Shakespeare's, and he was willing to make some allowance for their assertions. When, however, the Quartos are more closely examined Professor Tucker Brooke's concession shrinks into nothing at all; there is no evidence for assuming the existence of Marlowe originals for these defective Quartos other than 2 and 3 *Henry VI*; and if the Marlowe parallels prove anything about authorship it is that 2 and 3 *Henry VI* are by Marlowe.

It is unnecessary to return to *Richard Duke of York* and resume the trail of Warwick and Clifford: the main conclusion is clear. *The Contention* and *Richard Duke of York* are pirated versions of 2 and 3 *Henry VI*, put together by two of the leading players in Pembroke's Company, after the failure of the tour in 1593. These actors had in their possession certain manuscripts or portions of them; and they were no doubt helped in places by some of their fellows; but what they chiefly relied on was the memory, sometimes the possession, of their own parts, and the recollection of the plays as a whole that remained with them from frequent rehearsals and performances.

III. THE EARLY PLAYS OF THE SCHOOLMASTER FROM THE COUNTRY

MALONE'S argument to establish the dependence of 2 and 3 *Henry VI* on their respective Quartos breaks down under examination, for it misrepresents the facts. Two more texts can now be taken from the list of works regarded as pre-Shakespearean and added to the number of the Bad Quartos. The further consequences of the failure of Malone's argument become apparent when the question is considered how he fell into his error; for it is remarkable that so distinguished a Shakespearean scholar should at every turn in an argument so minute and extensive completely misinterpret the evidence. When we remember how Porson is said to have pronounced Malone's *Dissertation on Henry VI* one of the most convincing pieces of criticism he had ever met with, how it has given a bias to almost all subsequent comment on these texts, and how frequently it has been elaborated by succeeding scholars, it is clear that there lies behind Malone's conviction some strong prepossession. To discover this bias and understand how it drew him from the direct and plain line of the evidence, it is necessary to consider Malone's examination of the three parts of *Henry VI* in its place in the great critical effort to which he devoted himself, and which he carried through with such beneficial and lasting results to Shakespearean scholarship. This is the more necessary since his work when considered as a whole provides not merely the explanation of the particular errors so far discovered, but the only foundation for a more consistent judgment on these very texts themselves.

When he began his work on Shakespeare Malone found that the comparative value of the various ancient copies of Shakespeare's plays had not yet been precisely ascertained; that no biographical account with any pretence to critical method had yet appeared; and that no satisfactory attempt had been made to trace the order of the plays. All these gaps in Shakespearean criticism he attempted to make good. For the first he was able to use the work of previous editors; for the other two he had a great deal to do from the beginning. Rowe had indeed prefixed to his edition of the plays a life of Shakespeare, but his work here is as uncritical as that on the text. No one regarded his text as reliable or constructed on sound principles, but till Malone took up the question of the life Rowe's successors had been content in this with his account.[1] Dr Johnson afterwards added the story of Will. Shakespeare's boys, and this he gives as a story "which Mr Pope related as communicated to him by Mr Rowe"; it has therefore no more authority than the remainder of Rowe's anecdotes. Malone was the first to examine these traditions critically, and to institute that intensive search for and study of contemporary records bearing on Shakespeare's life and circumstances, by which he fixed the outline of the life as we know it, or should know it, to-day. And modern criticism owes him no less a debt for his third work, his attempt to ascertain

[1] All except Theobald who included some facts resting on documentary evidence discovered by Rymer.

the order in which the plays were written: such an inquiry provides the framework for any speculation on the development of the dramatist's art; and without Malone the bulk of nineteenth-century criticism would have no backbone at all.

But the very comprehensive nature of Malone's undertaking forced questions upon him which his predecessors could pass by or dismiss in the course of a paragraph. He had to answer such a question at the beginning of his study of the chronological order of the plays. It is raised by Rowe himself who wrote:

It would be without doubt a pleasure to any man, curious in things of this kind, to see and know what was the first essay of a fancy like Shakespeare's. Perhaps we are not to look for his beginnings, like those of other authors, among their least perfect writings; art had so little, and nature so large a share in what he did, that, for aught I know, the performances of his youth, as they were the most vigorous, and had the most fire and strength of imagination in them, were the best.

In justice to Rowe it should be noted that he shows a sounder judgment in particular instances. *The Tempest*, in his opinion,

however it comes to be placed the first by the publishers of his works, can never have been the first written by him: it seems to me as perfect in its kind, as almost anything we have of his.

But this observation and a note on *Henry V* and *Henry VIII* are his only contributions to the chronology. Rowe would have been pleased to learn which was the first play Shakespeare wrote, but for lack of this interesting information he filled out the paragraph with a paradox and passed to his next topic; his undertaking runs smoothly off undelayed by the importunate doubts of scholarship. Malone had set himself a sterner duty and was bound to offer some guess, or produce some evidence, about Shakespeare's earliest compositions. It was unfortunately at this decisive point that he failed to turn to full account his own painstaking labours. The difficulty of the situation is best appreciated by considering the condition in which he found it.

It was thought that Shakespeare had become a dramatist by accident; he had been chased from Stratford by Sir Thomas Lucy for poaching in Charlecote Park, and had been glad to find mean employment about one of the London playhouses; there his admirable wit soon distinguished him as a dramatist. This is Rowe's story, and Dr Johnson also refers to his flight to London "from the terror of a criminal prosecution"; he contributed the additional information that it was the excellence of his horse-holding at theatre doors that first brought his abilities to notice, and gained him higher employment inside the theatre.

Though now inside the theatre it is not clear how Shakespeare set about writing his plays. He had, according to Rowe, little schooling, and "we are to consider him as a man that lived in a state of almost universal licence and ignorance";[1] he was only able to write his plays because he "lived under a kind of mere light of nature".[1] This is admittedly a very slender equipment for so remarkable a task, and the more Shakespeare's ignorance is insisted upon the less sufficient it appears. It was Dr Farmer who at last reduced the tradition of Shakespeare's want of

[1] Rowe's *Life of Shakespeare.*

learning to demonstration. His plays, he argued in his famous essay, support the tradition that "Shakespeare's early life was incompatible with a course of education";[1] for all those passages in his works advanced to prove his knowledge of Greek and Latin authors, the only subject taught at Elizabethan grammar schools, are derived from translations. But Farmer is as insistent as Rowe that this was no disadvantage, for "he came out of Nature's hand like Pallas out of Jove's head, at full growth and mature".[2] This is the old story once more, though the wording is more rhetorical; but it is clear that even Dr Farmer, who was a very positive man, felt this theory required modification.

A number of plays containing classical allusions and quotations, which suggest that their author had some familiarity with Latin, are undoubtedly found among Shakespeare's collected works. This evidence Farmer had to discover a means of explaining away: Shakespeare could not in his opinion have written them as they stood; they must therefore be in part at least the work of other men. The early editors, Pope and Theobald, encouraged by Ravenscroft's statement that *Titus Andronicus* was only revised by Shakespeare, had ventured to pronounce certain other Folio plays of the same kind. Farmer following the fashion added to this list of works not entirely by Shakespeare those plays which did not agree with his theories.

Having professed to know so much Farmer could hardly refuse to explain how Shakespeare came to rewrite these plays, and why Heminge and Condell

[1] Preface to second edition of Farmer's *Essay*, 1767.
[2] Farmer's *Essay*. He is quoting Edward Young.

published them as his works. Shakespeare, he thought, made a beginning as a dramatist by revising the works of other men; but Farmer's opinion rests only on general considerations since he had neither the historical nor textual knowledge to make it good. In the absence of accurate information of this kind he merely assumed that the details would fit his argument. His treatment of *The Taming of the Shrew*, to be dealt with later, and the following passage are sufficient to illustrate his procedure:

Aulus Gellius informs us that some plays are ascribed absolutely to Plautus, which he only *re-touched* and *polished*; and this is undoubtedly the case with our author likewise. The revival of *Pericles*, which Ben Jonson calls *stale* and *mouldy*, was probably his earliest attempt in the Drama.[1]

Although Farmer cannot be blamed for knowing nothing of the date of Shakespeare's share in *Pericles*, he might have dwelt longer on the fact that Heminge and Condell did not include *Pericles* among Shakespeare's plays. The simple explanation, that they omitted it, because it was in part the work of another dramatist, does not seem to have occurred to him; for he makes no distinction between this work and those plays in the First Folio he classes with it. Without staying to explain why Heminge and Condell excluded the one while including the others Farmer extends the view he takes of *Pericles* to all those like 1 *Henry VI*, which he regards as "previous to our author".

At the beginning of his examination of *Henry VI* Malone mentions that before he started on his dissertation Farmer had expounded to him this view of Shakespeare's first efforts as a dramatist, but it is

[1] Farmer's *Essay*.

at the critical moment when he begins the chronological survey of the plays that Malone reveals most
unreservedly his reliance on Farmer. He assigns
first place in the line of plays to 1 *Henry VI*; 2 and
3 *Henry VI* follow, and he concludes his observations
on these two parts as follows:

Dr Farmer is of opinion, that Ben Jonson particularly
alludes in the following verses to our poet's having followed
the steps of Marlowe in the plays now under our consideration, and greatly *surpassed* his original:

> For, if I thought my judgment were of years,
> I should commit thee surely with thy peers;
> And tell how much thou didst our Lily *outshine*,
> Or sporting Kyd, or *Marlowe's* mighty line.

From the epithet *sporting*, which is applied to Kyd, and
which is certainly in some measure a quibble on his name,
it is manifest that he must have produced some *comick* piece
upon the scene, as well as the two tragedies of his composition which are now extant, *Cornelia*, and *The Spanish
Tragedy*. Dr Farmer, with great probability suggests to me,
that Kyd might have been the author of the old *Taming
of a Shrew* printed in 1594, on which Shakespeare formed
a play with nearly the same title. The praise which Ben
Jonson gives to Shakespeare, that he "*outshines* Marlowe
and Kyd", on this hypothesis, will appear to stand on one
and the same foundation; namely on his eclipsing those
ancient dramatists by new-modelling their plays, and
producing pieces much superior to theirs, on stories which
they had already formed into dramas, that, till Shakespeare
appeared, satisfied the publick, and were classed among the
happiest efforts of dramatick art. (Boswell's *Malone*, ii,
315.)

Farmer was not the first to find other hands than
Shakespeare's in the plays of the First Folio, but he

seems to have been the first to invent this explanation of how Shakespeare started on his dramatic career; and the theory arose[1] in his attempt to explain how Shakespeare, handicapped by his ignorance and mean upbringing, could make a start at all. He was, it seems, educated by the dramatists in whose works he played, till he was able to go beyond his masters; he first experimented on their work and then he wrote his own. How strongly Farmer was entrenched in this opinion is seen from his interpretation of Ben Jonson's lines. It is almost incredible that a critical mind should twist the simple statement that Shakespeare outshone Lily, Marlowe and Kyd, into evidence that Shakespeare rewrote their plays. But "every cold empiric", as Dr Johnson observed, "when his heart is expanded by a successful experiment, swells into a theorist, and the laborious collator at some unlucky moment frolicks in conjecture".

Once this theory had gained ground, it would not seem unnatural to those who were influenced by it if some of the dramatists who had instructed Shakespeare in his ignorance should envy him in his prosperity, and grudge him the popularity gained in revising their work. In Greene's address Malone thought he had discovered an attack by one of the senior dramatists capable of being interpreted in the light of the situation devised by Farmer for the young

[1] Not logically of course. The logical deduction from Farmer's premises will be found in *Elizabethan Drama and Dramatists*, by E. A. Gerrard, where the illiterate Shakespeare's first attempts at revision are found in *The Contention* and *Richard Duke of York*. These are what he is supposed to have made of the original works by Greene and Nashe, later printed as 2 and 3 *Henry VI*. This is the *reductio ad absurdum* of Farmer's theory.

Shakespeare. Once Farmer's hypothesis was confirmed, a safe beginning could be made on the
chronology, and the question answered which would
not be put by.

Malone's interpretation of Greene's letter stands
on the same footing as Farmer's interpretation of
Ben Jonson; at every turn he insists, contrary to
previous critical opinion and the obvious sense of the
words themselves, that Greene is accusing Shakespeare of plagiarism, and even pointing to the very
plays he revised; and in notes to almost every scene
of the plays Malone cites the most garbled Quarto
passages as the unmistakable originals of the corresponding parts in Shakespeare. Like Farmer he has
a thesis to support; for it is not saying too much for
Malone's critical ability that he would never have
made so many persistent errors, had he not been over
anxious to find the youthful Shakespeare in the very
act of rewriting the plays of his older contemporaries.
Nor can it be doubted that these errors would long
ago have been swept away, had not subsequent
criticism been hampered by the fact that what may
be called the deer-stealing-horse-holding-botching
theory fills a difficult gap that can hardly be left
vacant in the history of Shakespeare's life and art.

Farmer's theory that Shakespeare began by revising the work of others still holds the field, but it
now rests for support chiefly on Malone's textual
evidence. It is, however, an ironical turn of fortune
that unites them, for Malone had already proved that
this theory, which his textual evidence was framed to
support and which it does indeed still maintain,
originated in a mistaken idea of Farmer's, and was
designed to explain a situation that existed only in

the critic's fancy. Malone did not accept the deer-stealing and horse-holding stories, which are an essential part of Farmer's argument, and he proved that the idea that Shakespeare's early life was incompatible with a course of education is in direct conflict with all the positive evidence. To understand how Malone came to be the chief supporter of a theory he had demolished, it is necessary to consider separately the two parts which combine to form Farmer's theory, for it has a biographical and a textual element.

In his study of the poet's life Malone was able to show that Shakespeare had no need to flee to London for stealing Sir Thomas Lucy's deer at Charlecote, for Sir Thomas Lucy never had a deer park at that place or in the vicinity. The documentary evidence for this produced by Malone and Smart,[1] who completed the proof by a further study of the official records, is available because the regulations and warrants under which gentlemen were permitted to keep deer were enforced and recorded with great care. Further, the account Davies gives of the episode reveals a complete misconception of the procedure open to Sir Thomas Lucy had Shakespeare been a poacher.[1] On this decisive evidence the story goes to pieces; but it should be noted that the story itself satisfies none of the conditions that entitle a tradition to credit. These conditions Malone has stated in a general form which cannot be improved upon.

Where a tradition has been handed down, by a very industrious and careful inquirer, who has derived it from persons most likely to be accurately informed concerning

[1] *Shakespeare: Truth and Tradition*, by John S. Smart, pp. 95–97.

the fact related, and subjoins his authority, such a species of tradition must always carry great weight along with it.

But Rowe was not a very industrious and careful inquirer; nor do we know that he derived his information from anyone well informed concerning the matter, for he has not mentioned his authority, unless the deer-stealing story is part of the information which Betterton collected during his visit to Stratford. But more than twenty years before, Stratford had been visited by a much more industrious and careful inquirer than Betterton, and he heard nothing there but what is manifestly untrue. The local gossip collected in Stratford nearly a hundred years after Shakespeare's death is equally worthless.

The story no doubt originated in an attempt to reconstruct Shakespeare's biography from the plays; this particular episode is from *The Merry Wives of Windsor*. There Justice Shallow, who comes on complaining that Falstaff has robbed his deer park, seems (for the whole business is obscure) to have luces, a kind of fish, on his coat of arms. This point is emphasized for purposes of comedy by a punning allusion to the louse and the old coats on which it is sometimes to be found. But although the arms of Sir Thomas Lucy of Charlecote, as well as those of others, contain *luces*, there is nothing to show that this is anything but a mere coincidence; for Shallow is not a vindictive portrait of a man anything like the real Sir Thomas Lucy, or even the Sir Thomas of the tradition. As a portrait of the Stratford squire the character has no point whatever.[1] This is perhaps

[1] *Shakespeare: Truth and Tradition*, by John S. Smart, p. 97. *A Life of William Shakespeare*, by Joseph Quincy Adams, p. 84.

the first instance of a method in Shakespearean biography which has become very much more popular in our own time; but neither the modern instances nor this older example inspire any confidence in the method.

The horse-holding story is similarly without foundation. Dr Johnson noted that Pope related it as communicated to him by Rowe. As we have seen, this would not entitle it to belief. In Cibber's *Lives of the Poets*, however, Rowe is said to have had it from Betterton, who had it from Davenant. But this is no more than a guess, on the writer's part, of how it might have reached Rowe; for Shiels, who compiled the *Lives*, derived all he knew of the anecdote from Johnson himself, and Johnson says nothing of Rowe's sources. Such a remarkable story, hardly intelligible in view of many well-established facts about Shakespeare's circumstances, and not appearing till nearly 150 years after his death, requires before it can be accepted much better credentials than Dr Johnson was able to give it.

Malone rejected both these traditions, and showed that the general picture into which they were fitted, outlined by Rowe and taken for granted by Farmer, is absolutely untrustworthy. A boy brought up at a grammar school like that of Stratford, with its ancient standing and succession of able masters, Oxford graduates and frequently fellows of their colleges, was not necessarily ignorant; and if he had any memory and intelligence at all, since Latin was the one subject to which nearly all the time of a grammar school was given up, he of necessity read Latin with some facility. The composition of Latin epistles was also part of the regular grammar school curriculum, and does not seem to have been neglected at Stratford; for Malone actually quotes a Latin letter which Shakespeare's intimate friend Quiney received, when in London, from his son, a boy of ten or eleven. That Quiney read Latin easily other intimate letters from a friend bear evidence. But how it came about that Shakespeare should not have read Latin as easily as his friend and contemporary Quiney, or written it in his youth as fluently as Quiney's young son, are questions that have never been answered by those who assume with Farmer that his early life was incompatible with a course of education.

Malone failed to press home the conclusions that follow from this evidence, partly because he was diverted by his own idea that Shakespeare had been an attorney's clerk. His failure is the more disappointing, since there is one tradition that must be accepted before all the others, if any pretence is made to critical method. Among Aubrey's memoranda is the note:

Though, as Ben Jonson sayes of him, that he had but little Latine and lesse Greek, he understood Latine pretty well, for he had been in his younger yeares a schoolmaster in the countrey—from Mr Beeston.

This of course is the tradition most decisively rejected by Farmer and his school, but it is the only one that satisfies the three requirements laid down by Malone. It has been handed down by Aubrey, who was a very industrious and careful inquirer, who derived it from William Beeston, a person most likely to be accurately informed concerning the fact related, for he was an actor and manager and son of Christopher

Beeston, who had been one of Shakespeare's associates from 1594 to 1602; and Aubrey has subjoined
his authority by writing after this particular entry,
"from Mr Beeston".

It is instructive to observe the method Farmer
adopts for ridding himself of this awkward evidence,
as it reveals the shifts to which he was driven by his
thesis. He begins by an appeal to tradition, and quotes
Ben Jonson's "small Latine and lesse Greeke". To
interpret this he cites the adaptation of Ben Jonson's
words, "small Latin and *no* Greek", which was
used some thirty years later in a panegyric on Cart-
wright by Towers, and seems prepared to defend
this reading as a possible variant in Jonson's poem.
This is about as scholarly an emendation as the
substitution of *player's hide* for *woman's hide* would
be in 3 *Henry VI*, because Greene had quoted it in
that form. But to the comment on Jonson's words
by an intelligent and well-informed colleague he
attaches no weight whatsoever, because the remainder of Aubrey's evidence, he says, proves that
Shakespeare could not have been a schoolmaster.

As well as the information he obtained from
Beeston, Aubrey has recorded the following story:

His father was a butcher, and I have been told heretofore
by some of the neighbours that when he was a boy he
exercised his father's trade, but when he killd a calfe he
would doe it in a high style, and make a speech.

The first part of this information as well as the
second Aubrey obtained "from some of the neighbours" during a visit to Stratford; for they told him
about the killing of the calves and his following his
father in business. The first part is of course incorrect

as Farmer pointed out; by what mental processes he goes on to insist that, because the first statement is incorrect, the second undoubtedly proves that Shakespeare never was a schoolmaster, it is impossible to say; unless we suppose he had some private satisfaction in choosing to believe the one and not the other, sharing, possibly, what Wordsworth has called "the too common propensity of human nature" of wishing to have some advantage over "a genius whom he had been compelled to regard with admiration, as an inmate of the celestial regions—'there sitting where he durst not soar'".

Nor does it follow, as Farmer implies, that because Aubrey jotted down in his memoranda, which he never put in order for publication, discrepant statements that he is unworthy of credit. He has recorded what he was told, and the value of the evidence depends on the witness who gave it; nor does his superstition, which Farmer insists upon, in any way affect the veracity of his records. Malone quotes the evidence of a trustworthy contemporary[1] that he "was superstitious...yet most accurate in his account of matters of fact", and adds the weight of his own knowledge and judgment by saying that Aubrey's character for veracity had never been impeached.[2]

Aubrey's memoranda leave us to choose between the evidence of William Beeston, whose ability and honesty is attested by his contemporaries, and who

[1] Farmer omits to say that the contemporary whose spiteful comment he quotes was the man who owed most to Aubrey's accuracy.

[2] See *Shakespeare: Truth and Tradition*, by John S. Smart, pp. 85–7; and Boswell's *Malone*, II, 696.

through his father was in a position to know the facts
he related, and the story of some Stratford gossip
whom Aubrey questioned about the year 1680, and
who told him what is, in part at least, untrue.

It is indeed a fact that Halliwell-Phillipps preferred the story that Shakespeare was a butcher, but
fortunately he has put on record the principles on
which he made his choice. "In the compilation of the
following pages", he says in his *Outlines*, "it has been
thought advisable, in estimating the authority of the
various traditions, to give the preference, wherever
selection was necessary, to the rural versions."
Secure in this simple faith he never mentions
Beeston's statement in the body of his narrative, and
merely remarks in a note,

It is very unlikely that there can be any truth in Aubrey's
unsupported statement, and it is, indeed, inconsistent with
what Aubrey himself previously observes respecting
Shakespeare's early life.

Since Aubrey's statement is supported by the name
of Beeston, it is clear that Halliwell-Phillipps did not
give the note sufficient consideration, and that his
further objection is made without reflection. To
allow the evidence of a judicious colleague to be
outweighed even by a whole countryside of gossips
would be a weakness on the part of the biographer;
to accept every idle story from the country as Halliwell-
Phillipps has done is to make biography the chronicle
of the ale-house. He at least could plead that he was
a Wordsworthian, and that his faith in rural versions
and distrust of those from the town expressed his
belief in what he thought, however mistakenly, was
that poet's teaching: those who are misled by

Halliwell-Phillipps can seldom offer so acceptable an excuse.

It is now safe to say of the biographical part of the theory we are examining that it is without foundation, and that if we know anything about Shakespeare's employment between his leaving school and entering the theatre it is that he was a schoolmaster in the country.

In passing to question the textual part of the theory we no longer have Malone's support. Where the chronological study of the plays begins the biographical and textual evidence join; Malone had provided the material for closing the biographical gap, which for want of positive knowledge had been filled with Restoration gossip; he failed to sweep away the remaining rubbish that stood in the way of a sound chronology, for lack of one decisive piece of textual information. Lacking this he had recourse to traditions and guesses as crumbling and undependable as those he rejected from the biography, and allowed the theory he had half demolished to rise again. In spite of all his labour on the problem of the comparative value of the various ancient copies of Shakespeare's plays, he still retained what had become the accepted view, that the text, however good, had come down to us through the offices of piratical publishers and unscrupulous editors. The following passage from his Preface summarizes these views:

With respect to [the quartos with good texts] though undoubtedly they were all surreptitious, that is, stolen from the playhouse, and printed without the consent of the author or the proprietors, they *in general* are preferable to the exhibition of the same plays in the folio; for this plain reason, because, instead of printing these plays from a manuscript, the editors of the folio, to save labour, or from some other motive, printed the greater part of them from the very copies which they represented as maimed and imperfect, and frequently from a late, instead of the earliest edition.

A text that depends more on the thieving of pirates than the honesty of its editors is one that might provoke considerable speculation in the most conservative of commentators.

But in the volume which stands at the head of this series of studies on the text Professor Pollard has proved Malone's criticism of Heminge and Condell unfounded and misleading. Like the earlier editors Malone misunderstood the passage in the address "To the great Variety of Readers" on which this unfavourable judgment rests; for Heminge and Condell's words, "stolne and surreptitious copies", were not intended, as he thought, to describe all the previous editions of Shakespeare's plays, but only a small and particular class of publication. The early editions published before 1623 are, as Professor Pollard has demonstrated, of two kinds, Good Quartos and Bad Quartos; and the terms *good* and *bad* cover more than the mere quality of the texts, and take account of factors in their transmission from Shakespeare's manuscript to the printed page hitherto uninvestigated. The Bad Quartos are the "stolne and surreptitious copies" to which Heminge and Condell refer; against these alone they make their protest. It follows that their statement,

where (before) you were abus'd with diuerse stolne, and surreptitious copies, maimed, and deformed by the frauds and stealthes of iniurious impostors, that expos'd them:

euen those, are now offer'd to your view cur'd, and perfect of their limbes;

gives a fair and true account of their editorial care. They provided genuine texts of the plays which had so far appeared only in Bad Quartos. These they superseded; but they make no reflection on the authenticity of the Good Quartos, some of which they wisely reprinted; and such reprinting in no way detracts from their competence or good faith. By this one vital distinction between Good Quartos and Bad Quartos Professor Pollard has put an end to the idea that the text is desperately discased. The desperate remedies so freely prescribed for its amendment must now give place to more natural treatment.

The important consequences of this discovery can best be appreciated by considering how Malone's statements must now be modified. His assertion that all the Quartos are surreptitious, that is stolen from the playhouse and printed without the consent of the author or the proprietors, has been replaced by the view that certain of these early texts were printed from manuscript supplied by the Company or by Shakespeare himself. No doubt the copy was frequently in Shakespeare's own handwriting. The authority therefore of some of these early editions is very much greater than even Malone suspected; and this Professor Dover Wilson has emphasized in his work on the text.

A second consequence, however, just as decisive has not yet been so fully recognized. It is admitted that Malone's charge, that Heminge and Condell to save labour, or from some other motive, printed from the very copies which they represented as maimed and imperfect, cannot now be sustained.

The further complaint that they reprinted from late
instead of the earliest copies is of course well founded,
but this does not impeach their good faith; more
especially when we take into account the laborious
collation with the playhouse manuscripts which these
late Quartos underwent. It is therefore no longer
possible to represent Heminge and Condell as de-
ceiving the public and on that score to cast doubts
on information resting on their word. Their text
itself has to be studied as the honest and painstaking
effort of men who, though not expert bibliographers,
were well informed, and who by the very choice of
the Quartos they reprinted showed their knowledge
as well as their limitations. It was natural for editors
who felt their taste superior to Shakespeare's own to
regard his fellows as ignorant and unreliable. When
Steevens says he sometimes followed the suggestions
of a Warburton, a Johnson, a Farmer, or a Tyrwhitt
in preference to the decisions of a Heminge or a
Condell, he shows the same arrogance and ignorance
he displayed in his judgment on the Sonnets;[1] and
his licence in dealing with textual detail is as unsound
and impertinent as his criticism. But in a matter
where the actual knowledge of Heminge and Condell
is more plainly preserved than in the textual detail
of the First Folio, being unobscured by technical
difficulties, we still accept the suggestions of a
Farmer and a Steevens in preference to the decisions

[1] We have not reprinted the Sonnets, because the strongest
act of parliament that could be framed would fail to compel
readers into their service. Had Shakespeare produced no other
works than these, his name would have reached us with as little
celebrity as time has conferred on that of Thomas Watson, an
older and much more elegant sonneteer.

of Shakespeare's associates. Their inclusion of certain plays in the Folio is by many writers hardly regarded as of any weight in determining whether these works are by Shakespeare or by others. But with Professor Pollard's conclusions in mind we are entitled to demand from any critic, who ascribes parts and plays in the Folio to other dramatists than Shakespeare, unequivocal evidence for his opinion. It will no longer do to ignore the statement of the first editors that they had collected *his* plays "to keepe the memory of so worthy a Friend, and Fellow aliue, as was our SHAKESPEARE".

Malone, however, was still infected with the traditional mistrust of Heminge and Condell. He considered he had clear proof that they were untrustworthy, and he did not question as closely as was usual with him the evidence for the long-accepted opinion that they included much that was not by Shakespeare. Just however as the horse-holding deer-stealing stories proved on examination to be Restoration gossip, the statement which lies behind the view that Heminge and Condell included plays only touched by Shakespeare is a story of the same period; and this time it has all the marks of a deliberate invention.

In 1687 Ravenscroft when printing his version of *Titus Andronicus* said in his preface:

I have been told by some anciently conversant with the Stage, that it was not Originally his, but brought by a private Author to be Acted, and he only gave some Master-touches to one or two of the Principal Parts or Characters; this I am apt to believe, because 'tis the most incorrect and indigested piece in all his Workes, It seems rather a heap of Rubbish than a Structure.

When this account is examined for the three marks which, as Malone indicated, point to a good tradition, it is clear that two at least are missing. In the first place Ravenscroft cannot be regarded as a careful and industrious inquirer. He was taking the liberty of altering a greater man's work, and, though this was also done by those who should have known better than Ravenscroft, there were not wanting judgments whose censure he had to face. The tradition which he produced enabled him to meet this in some measure; but his contemporary, Langbaine, did not hesitate to charge him with inventing it for the purpose. It is clear from Ravenscroft's Prologue that, when his version was first performed, he had no doubt he was rewriting the work of Shakespeare; he had ventured to say, as Langbaine reminded him,

> So far he was from robbing him of's Treasure,
> That he did add his own, to make full Measure.

His later assertion that the play was not Shakespeare's has all the appearance of an after-thought, suggested by reflection on his effrontery in the Prologue, which he now declared was lost. Nor does it help to argue that he might have had this information from Beeston, or some equally good authority. He may, or he may not. What we know is that he did not give the name of his informant, when this was all that was required to silence his critic.

But *Titus Andronicus* itself, it is frequently asserted, is sufficient evidence that the work is not by Shakespeare. This statement raises the whole question on what grounds we are entitled to set aside the evidence of Heminge, Condell, and Meres. Farmer main-

tained that his idea of Shakespeare's early days
enabled him to check their assertions, and reject what
did not harmonize with his conceptions. When
certain scenes and even plays were removed the
remainder of the work in the Folio could be, he
seemed to think, attributed without improbability to
the uneducated deer-stealer. But his theory is surmise
and his criticism therefore worthless. What basis the
aesthetic argument against *Titus* can have it is unnecessary to inquire, till someone has been able to
indicate it with something like completeness. Meantime it is sufficient to observe that those plays in the
Folio for which an early date can be fixed (they
include *Titus*), and which may therefore be expected
to reveal most clearly Shakespeare's early tastes and
studies, confirm in a remarkable manner the one
trustworthy tradition about his youthful employment.
The early plays are what might be expected from a
schoolmaster turned dramatist.

An Elizabethan schoolmaster would naturally find
his early models in Latin authors; and this is where
Shakespeare found his. An early comedy, probably
his first, is *The Comedy of Errors*, adapted from the
Menaechmi of Plautus. Farmer's observation that
his immediate source was Warner's translation is a
mere guess since the translation appeared later than
the comedy; and it is wasting time to argue against
the assumption that Shakespeare may have seen the
translation in manuscript, for he drew his material
from the *Amphitruo* as well, of which no translation
is known to have been available. Shakespeare's
acquaintance with yet another of the comedies of
Plautus, the *Mostellaria*, is suggested by his transference of the names of the town and country slaves,

Tranio and Grumio, to the servants in *The Taming of the Shrew.*

Shakespeare's first tragedy is *Titus Andronicus.* Some reject it as too horrible to be his, others as too learned, because it includes, as well as many classical quotations, an allusion to the *Ajax* of Sophocles. But Seneca, whose work provided the model for this tragedy of blood and revenge, has furnished his imitator with suggestions for most of the strong situations; and the closing horror, the serving of Tamora with the baked flesh of her children, is straight from the *Thyestes.* Nor can it be said of Seneca that he wrote down to a mob whose applause he hoped to win with his crude horrors, for his plays were written for a select circle well versed in the Greek masters in whose steps he followed. If Seneca is no mere crude sensationalist, neither is his imitator; and the view that *Titus Andronicus* is nothing more than an appeal to the groundlings is entirely lacking in historical perspective. It is a tragedy founded in part on the classical story of Philomela and Tereus; it draws largely on Senecan situations, and is freely embellished with classical allusions and quotations. It is true it does not seem so classical to-day as it did no doubt to its author, but this is true of Seneca himself and all Elizabethan imitations of the classics. Classical scholarship has altered the general outlook since Sidney commended Seneca to his contemporaries. But *Titus Andronicus* is certainly written in an unvulgar style, and everything including the quotations favours its ascription to the youthful schoolmaster.

Shakespeare's first poem is *Venus and Adonis,* another work suggested by his Latin reading. Once more historical knowledge is required to realize how it appealed to contemporaries. Ovid is his model, and Ovid no longer holds the place in the admiration of classical students he had in Elizabethan England. This change is part of a greater change in outlook; and there is little doubt that, if Shakespeare's name did not stand on the title page of this poem, there would not be wanting critics ready to assign it to some other poet. They have dismissed *Titus Andronicus* from the canon, although it is linked to this poem by many internal marks of style, subject matter, and treatment; most arguments against *Titus* can be applied with equal force to *Venus and Adonis*. The poem, however, cannot be explained away, and it clearly agrees with the tradition that in his youth Shakespeare was a schoolmaster, not with the view that he came to London with everything to seek.

The classical quotations, allusions, and borrowings, in the early plays, so far from proving that Heminge and Condell were printing work which was not by Shakespeare, increase our confidence in the integrity of their text. The one authentic tradition of the early years and the textual tradition agree that what Farmer declared was certainly not Shakespeare's could indeed be his; Beeston said Shakespeare was a schoolmaster, Heminge and Condell published as his what has all the marks of this schooling. Both traditions come from Shakespeare's own Company and they confirm each other. To believe that the casual gossips of Stratford eighty or a hundred years after Shakespeare's death knew as much about him, or cared as much what they said of him, as his colleagues is a strange credulity, only matched by the scepticism with which the same hearers receive the testimony of his fellows. Those who believe there was no conspiracy in Shakespeare's Company to delude posterity, and know how idle stories grow round great names when their history is left uncared for, need not remain in doubt about Shakespeare's beginnings as a dramatist. They have to choose between the rural versions from which the speculations of the Farmer school are derived, and the evidence of Shakespeare's three colleagues, Beeston, Heminge, and Condell.

The theory which would incline us to look for the work of other hands in Shakespeare's early plays has neither biographical nor textual foundation. There are a number of anonymous Quartos—*The Contention, Richard Duke of York, The Taming of a Shrew, The Troublesome Reign of King John, The Famous Victories of Henry V*, and *The True Chronicle History of King Leir*—which have been represented as the material Shakespeare actually made use of. How much support the Quartos of 2 and 3 *Henry VI* give this theory has been estimated in some of the earlier pages; *The Taming of a Shrew* has been dealt with elsewhere.[1] The others do not affect the present argument. Shakespeare's *King John*, 1 and 2 *Henry IV*, *Henry V*, and *King Lear*, are not considered among his early works. The rehandling of old material by an acknowledged master is not improbable, and quite distinct from a beginner's revision of the work of established dramatists. Further the Folio versions of these plays contain hardly a line found in their supposed originals; their Quartos therefore do not

[1] *The Times Literary Supplement*, 16 September 1926. See especially the Cambridge "New Shakespeare" edition of *The Taming of the Shrew*, p. 105.

stand in the relation to Shakespeare's text which it was thought *The Contention* and *Richard Duke of York* did to 2 and 3 *Henry VI*. Heminge and Condell cannot be shown to have included in the Folio whole scenes in the very words of other men.

Those who rely on internal evidence in ascribing any Folio play to some of Shakespeare's contemporaries have now to depend entirely on the strength of their particular argument; they cannot claim support from any well-established theory that other plays in the collection are undoubtedly of this origin, or that their assumptions are in keeping with a reasonable view of the conditions in which Shakespeare began his work as a dramatist. They have also to reconcile their claim with the fact that Heminge and Condell, though they excluded *Pericles*, included the play in question; and, to return to 1, 2, 3 *Henry VI* and *Richard III*, that Greene as well as Heminge and Condell thought 3 *Henry VI* by Shakespeare, and that Meres entered *Richard III* in his list of the poet's works.

IV. THE ALTERNATIVE TO
HEMINGE AND CONDELL

THOSE who are prepared to accept the argument offered to them in the preceding pages, but who still maintain that 2 and 3 *Henry VI*, though included in the First Folio, are not entirely by Shakespeare, must now rely, unless they think their proposition self evident, on evidence similar to that advanced by Professor Tucker Brooke. They can no longer assume with Farmer that Shakespeare came to London all but illiterate, and that he must have made a start as a dramatist by tinkering the plays of others; nor like Malone can they reject the traditions on which this view is formed, and still point to Greene's quotation from 3 *Henry VI*, and to *The Contention* and *Richard Duke of York*, as proof that though the butcher of Farmer's story must go the botcher may remain. Nor is it any longer possible to represent Heminge and Condell as handing down to posterity a considerable number of the plays in versions which are no more than the compilations of piratical publishers, and so disregard their authority. Professor Pollard has once for all vindicated the integrity of their work; where they had been thought most to offend they were, he has shown, only reprinting texts which may very well have been set up from Shakespeare's own manuscripts. Those therefore who challenge the statement of Heminge and Condell that they were publishing Shakespeare's "owne writings" must rely entirely on the particular evidence they can

bring forward; they can look for no support from
any general considerations drawn from Shakespeare's
upbringing and education or from the dishonesty of
his editors.

It has frequently been assumed that the Folio was
a composite production, the work of many dramatists,
and that all a critic who questioned the authorship of
any particular play had to do was to read through the
works of the many Elizabethans, produce some
parallel of thought, diction, or style, from one of their
plays, and conclude that this man also contributed to
Shakespeare's works. The coincidences frequently
selected, even by the best at this game, commonly
prove on examination of no substance whatever; but,
even if these were as convincing as their discoverers
claim, they derive almost all their force from being
joined to the notion that some of the First Folio plays
are demonstrably from other hands. This assumption
can no longer be maintained. And since in the circumstances in which Elizabethan drama was produced coincidences of all kinds are inevitable, what
is required is a coincidence, or a congeries of coincidences, which when taken by itself is of sufficient
force to put aside the testimony of Shakespeare's
friends; and, if the question is of some of the Good
Quartos, what amounts to the testimony of Shakespeare himself that he was the author. Facts which
suggest some alien hand in the text as a possible, or
even plausible, explanation of their being are not
sufficient; they must be such that the conclusion
they point to is unavoidable, otherwise there is no
reasonable alternative to thinking that Heminge and
Condell meant what they said, and that the work is
Shakespeare's.

(i) 2 and 3 *Henry VI*

The parallels with *Edward II* in 2 or 3 *Henry VI*,
collected by Professor Tucker Brooke, are not when
taken by themselves proof that Marlowe was the
author of these plays; and it is only fair to note that
Professor Tucker Brooke did not intend his quotations to stand alone. For him they were only part of
an argument that relied on the assumption that 2 and
3 *Henry VI* were clearly revisions by Shakespeare of
another's work; he thought he had only to identify
the original author. It has been shown, however, that
2 and 3 *Henry VI* cannot be separated from their
Quartos as he premises, and that, if he has proved
Marlowe the author of the substance of *The Contention*
and *Richard Duke of York*, he has at the same time
proved that 2 and 3 *Henry VI* are his work. These
parallels therefore now lie alone in the scale against
Shakespeare's authorship, and few probably will be
willing to trust for a decision to their weight. It is
now all or nothing: Marlowe is either the author of
the whole of 2 and 3 *Henry VI* or there is no room
for him here at all.

If the conclusion to be maintained about the correct
procedure in such a choice is sound, Marlowe must
be excluded, for there are two other reasonable
explanations of the parallel passages: Marlowe may
have known 2 and 3 *Henry VI* and reproduced lines
or phrases consciously or unconsciously when writing
Edward II, or Shakespeare may be the imitator.[1]

----

[1] One has also to remember that *The Massacre at Paris* and
The Jew of Malta are only preserved in what Professor Tucker
Brooke regards as corrupt texts. The corrupters may have
introduced tags from *Henry VI*.

None of the parallels is of a kind to rule out these possibilities, since the closest are no more than isolated tags or unimportant phrases; nor is their number an objection, when those peculiar to the Quartos are set aside. Shakespeare was indeed the actor, and more likely to have reason to know by heart the plays of other men, but in the concluding chapter, where the connection between Marlowe and Shakespeare in Pembroke's Company is discussed, the view is put forward that Marlowe was following Shakespeare. For the moment the important point to establish is that, on the available evidence, one of these alternatives must be preferred to the theory that Marlowe wrote 2 and 3 *Henry VI*, if we are to maintain that the question admits of a reasoned answer.

Those who venture to think differently, and boldly put aside Heminge and Condell because of the coincidences between 2 or 3 *Henry VI* and *Edward II*, must be warned that on their own reckoning Professor Tucker Brooke is himself starting from a very insecure basis. If the attributions attached to good texts, issued in circumstances which give rise to no suspicion, are to be valueless as evidence, what right has anyone to assume that *Edward II* is by Marlowe? It was first published after his death, and there is not even a friendly preface to say the work is his, only a name on the title page. To the sceptic, however, this is no more than a publisher's fancy, and Mr J. M. Robertson finds evidence for assigning part at least of the play to Peele. This requires investigation by those who arguing from *Edward II* have found Marlowe in 2 and 3 *Henry VI*; for it may be Peele's work they have discovered there.

This is only the beginning of the difficulty. There

are, according to Mr Crawford,[1] at least thirty parallels with *Edward II* in *Arden of Feversham,* and some are as unmistakable as any in 2 or 3 *Henry VI.* It is true that it has been assumed that *Arden* is by Kyd, and that he is echoing Marlowe, but there is no evidence except the parallels themselves for dating *Arden* after *Edward II.* Those who insist that the parallels in 2 or 3 *Henry VI* are proof of Marlowe's hand must first decide whether Marlowe had a share in *Arden,* or Kyd in *Edward II.* This, however, does not bring us to the end of the difficulty. The ascription of *Arden* to Kyd is doubtful, and is maintained only by parallels between it and plays commonly assigned to Kyd; but the plays of Kyd, even *The Spanish Tragedy,* have no guarantee attached to them that they are entirely, or even in part, his work. Here again investigation must start afresh. Those who assign 2 and 3 *Henry VI* to Marlowe, on the evidence of Professor Tucker Brooke's list of quotations, are bound, if they wish to present a complete or consistent case, to pass from play to play till they have gone the round of nearly every dramatist of that time. This is what Mr J. M. Robertson, it seems, has set out to do in *The Shakespeare Canon;* and nothing less is required of those who assign 2 and 3 *Henry VI* to Marlowe on the strength of Professor Tucker Brooke's list of parallels.

But the method which those who ignore Heminge and Condell must propose to themselves has a defect which even the most industrious can never overcome. The journey on which their own arguments conduct them may not seem beyond their endurance and knowledge, but having passed from

[1] *Collectanea,* I, p. 100.

play to play till they have completed the full circle of parallel quotations in Elizabethan drama, they can only end in a whirl of surmise; for what means remains to them of distinguishing between one author and another in this obscurity where each seems either? Verse tests, tests of style, or structure, or substance, cannot help, for their use implies familiarity with a considerable body of work which is positively known to be by the particular author whose style is for the moment in question, a body of work from which the tests proposed may be clearly deduced. Wanting this, Mr J. M. Robertson and those condemned to pass with him from play to play must move in an infinite regress that can conduct them nowhere.

Mr Robertson's insistence upon the importance of his tests is perhaps a half-recognition of the real difficulty of his position. To simplify the question, merely for the sake of clear illustration, let us ask how these tests can help him to decide which are Shakespeare's early works, and how he proposes to escape the following dilemma?

Before he can apply his verse tests to work of this period Mr Robertson must first have studied a definite body of material from which they can be formulated, and this basic material, which alone can give positive value to his tests, he must have some positive reason for considering as Shakespeare's early work. Neither his own impressions nor any of his other tests afford any positive guidance in discovering this primary material; for he cannot know what tests will serve to discover Shakespeare's style till he is familiar with Shakespeare's actual work. Where has he found this work, and on whose authority does he claim it as Shakespeare's? For those who like

Mr Robertson set aside Heminge and Condell, and the ascriptions on Quartos recognized as Good, there can be no positive basis on which to frame any tests at all. None of his tests can acquire any positive character, or confer it on any other test, till he has something positive to begin with.

There is indeed an alternative, but it is one very repugnant to Mr Robertson's principles. He might claim that his tests have value because they formulate his own conceptions of what Shakespeare's early verse and style should be; and although his principles would doubtless compel him to deny any worth to such conceptions are not these what really guide him in practice? He objects, for example, to any play by Shakespeare being dated before *A Midsummer Night's Dream* that has much more than 7 per cent. of double endings; if the play with a higher percentage is known to be before that date, then someone other than Shakespeare is responsible for the double endings. But *A Midsummer Night's Dream* was probably written towards the end of the first period, or the beginning of the second, when Shakespeare's work on his poems may have given a new direction to his dramatic verse. How then can it guide us to the detail of his earlier verse? What calculus has been invented that would enable a student of *Paradise Lost* to reckon the kind of elisions Milton permitted himself in his earlier blank verse, or who after reading *Lamia* could tell how Keats must have handled the couplet two years before in his *Endymion*? This is what Mr Robertson does for Shakespeare. But Shakespeare's work before the poetic period may very well have a higher percentage of double endings; these may diminish in numbers for a time, and again increase, without exciting surprise except in one who has framed a theory of how it must have been.

If Mr Robertson should claim that the poet will at least show in his practice some consistency, this will be admitted; but he has to prove that the conception of poetic consistency that underlies his numerical tests is applicable to the work of Shakespeare. Mr Robertson refuses to regard the first two scenes of *The Comedy of Errors* as by the same author, because one has a much higher percentage of double endings than the other. One, however, contains the solemn eloquence of a law court, the other the witty exchanges of the market place, and why should Shakespeare not have made a contrast? That he obtains similar contrasts elsewhere by different means is no objection. Further, that a play which as a whole shows about 12 per cent. of double endings cannot contain scenes which pass from 2 per cent. to 24 per cent. of this variety of line is not proved to be the least improbable by the statistics Mr Robertson submits. Although we may know the averages of the leading batsmen during the season, we cannot tell how often or by how much their consecutive innings may vary. What Mr Robertson has to work out are figures that will enable us to estimate the probability of these variations, and that is not to be done by the elementary process of striking a simple arithmetical average, and treating any marked deviations from it as impossible. This is not merely to misinterpret poetry, it is to misunderstand the methods of statistics. So far that subtlest of human phenomena, poetry, has only been subjected to a process of counting that gives results too crude to be called statistics; to tabulate and apply the true statistics of Shakespeare's verse will involve the most refined processes of calculation. Meantime the simple addition and division of the verse tests hitherto developed and their crude applications need not shake our confidence in Heminge and Condell.

Before Mr Robertson can challenge the consistency of the verse given us as Shakespeare's, he must first give consistency to his calculation of probabilities by putting it on a sound mathematical basis. It is possible to discern general trends in the development of Shakespeare's style and versification, but the minute discriminations which Mr Robertson makes the basis of much of his work merely arise from his own preconceptions. They are not even developed consistently, that is mathematically, from the available figures, and they cannot be accepted as based on an examination of what is actually Shakespeare's work; for Mr Robertson has offered no positive proof that he has yet been able to distinguish Shakespeare's plays from those of any other Elizabethan dramatist.

The difficulties of Mr Robertson's position cannot be passed over as those peculiar to an extreme type of criticism. Few force themselves full on the dilemma with Mr Robertson's inexorable logic, but it is only the critical inconstancy of many which saves them from his predicament. In his lecture to the British Academy in 1924 Sir Edmund Chambers has already outlined the dilemma here presented. He pointed out that Mr Robertson's clues from vocabulary and phraseology would be more sure, if we knew more clearly what each of Shakespeare's contemporaries wrote, and did not write. The mistake of assuming that the evidence on Good Shakespeare Quartos and in the Folio itself may be set aside while the plays of others need not be questioned is a common fallacy. Mr Robertson, however, professes to understand this, although when he talks of the unsigned works of Marlowe he seems to imply that he also had signed works, and the question suggests itself, What then are the signed plays of Shakespeare? Mr Robertson, indeed, recognizes the difficulty without being able to show how it may be overcome. In his reply to Sir Edmund Chambers, spread over his recent Shakespeare writings, he has found no satisfactory defence to this particular objection, except the retort that Sir Edmund is himself guilty of what he finds fault with in others. Mr Robertson maintains that he is only carrying on with more system than usual the practice of much orthodox scholarship, including that of Sir Edmund himself; and that what Malone and Farmer have sown he has reaped.[1]

The contention is a fair one, and cannot be answered while we stand one foot on sea and one on shore, denying to Shakespeare on the one hand *Titus Andronicus*, or *Henry VI*, while accepting *Romeo and Juliet*, or *Troilus* as his. Mr Robertson can give as plausible reasons for *his* particular choice as those who cling to the orthodox division. To slight the ascriptions found on "good" dramatic publications, and ignore the guidance of Heminge and Condell, is to have taken the first step into what Sir Edmund Chambers has called "the Robertsonian morass". Sir Edmund has himself, according to Mr Robertson, gone the length of disintegrating nine or eleven of Shakespeare's plays, and cannot be considered to have avoided all the dangers of the slough, however carefully he has picked his steps. And if he is in it who is not? To avoid the danger we must retrace our

[1] *The Shakespeare Canon*, Part III, p. 88.

steps, and regain the plain path indicated to us by the
Good Quartos and the First Folio.

The choice whether we are to desert this road
because of the quotations collected by Professor
Tucker Brooke is a momentous one, but not very
difficult when we realize where the bypath leads us.
It is clear that when a good alternative explanation
is open to us in such a difficulty we must not deny
to Shakespeare any one of the thirty-six plays in the
First Folio. The theory that 2 and 3 *Henry VI* are
by Greene, or Peele, or Marlowe, or anyone but
Shakespeare, has no textual foundation; the parallels
with *Edward II* are more simply accounted for by
another explanation than that advanced by Professor
Tucker Brooke. We need have no hesitation therefore in attributing 2 and 3 *Henry VI* to Shakespeare
himself.

(ii) *Richard III*

The solution of the problem presented to students
of Shakespeare by 2 and 3 *Henry VI* turns on discovering the true relationship between these plays
and their Bad Quartos. The problem of *Richard III*
is different but in some ways even more critical: the
relationship on which everything now depends is that
between the Folio and a Good Quarto. The Good
Quartos do not all give equally satisfactory texts.
There can be little doubt that some are straight from
Shakespeare's own manuscript, handed by the dramatist or his representative to the printer; and he was
prompted to see that certain of his works were
printed in this way from good copy by the very
imperfect versions which unscrupulous publishers had

passed off on the book market. Not all the Good Quartos are of this prime importance; it is probable that some of them were obtained by importunate publishers when it was inconvenient for the Company to part with the best or fullest version in their possession. But whatever the precise nature of the copy for a Good Quarto, marked differences between such a text and the corresponding version in the Folio demand careful study from those who insist on the authority of Heminge and Condell. Nothing could weaken the case for them so much as the admission that their text differed so markedly from that of a Good Quarto that the variants were to be explained only by supposing that another dramatist, as well as Shakespeare, had a share in the play. No Good Quarto differs so much from its Folio counterpart as that of *Richard III*, and the divergence has been taken as proof of divided authorship.

Once Malone had, as it seemed, solved the textual problem of 2 and 3 *Henry VI* and their respective Quartos by assuming that the real difficulty arose from the presence of other hands than Shakespeare's in these plays, it was almost inevitable that this explanation should be extended to *Richard III*. The more intensively the variants in the Quarto and Folio versions of the play were studied, the more perplexing appeared the relation of the texts. This culminated in the work of the first Cambridge editors, who declared, after their collation of the eight Quarto and four Folio texts, that

the respective origin and authority of the first Quarto and first Folio texts of *Richard III* is perhaps the most difficult question which presents itself to an editor of Shakespeare.

In this difficulty they propounded an elaborate scheme of textual relationships. Their own text, however, provides the most effective reply to their speculations; their criticism of their documents gave them no assured means of dealing with the many variants they contain, and cannot therefore be the necessary conclusion from the evidence at their disposal. Conscious no doubt of this, as well as of the labour they had spent on the tangle, they conclude with a statement which must come to the ears of those who venture to question their judgments with something of an oracular note:

We commend a study of the text of *Richard III* to those, if such there be, who imagine that it is possible by the exercise of critical skill to restore with certainty what Shakespeare actually wrote.

Already their theory attributes part of the confusion to the intervention of another hand than Shakespeare's; this indeed is only that of a transcriber with literary theories of his own; these he put in practice, they thought, when copying Shakespeare's *revised* draft of the play which they considered was the basis for the Folio. The Quarto, they concluded, contained Shakespeare's original version. Every theory of course must make some allowance for the interference of a transcriber, or a printer, or a stage manager going about his work as intelligently as may be, but the transcriber in this instance has become a literary agent whose mechanical task can provide no clue to his deliberate alterations; his work could be identified only by considerations such as might apply if another hand had intervened in the course of composition.

When Daniel took up the problem some years later, in his introduction to the facsimile by Griggs, he reversed the order of the texts proposed by the Cambridge editors, and maintained that "the Folio represents the play as first set forth by Shakespeare; the Quarto a shortened and revised copy of it". But he now took for granted that "it was not of Shakespeare's original composition but the work of the author or authors of the *Henry VI* series of plays". He did not consider, however, that this complicated what was for him the main question, the relation of the Quarto and Folio texts. These he examined without reference to the authorship of the play itself; but in his admirable analysis he finds it difficult to explain what is on his own admission one of the chief puzzles presented by the texts.

Any acceptable theory about the text of *Richard III* must explain the presence in the Quarto of the famous "clock" passage, which is not found in the Folio version (Act iv, sc. ii) of Richard's snub to Buckingham:

Buck.   What sayes your Highnesse to my iust request?
Rich.   I doe remember me, *Henry* the Sixt
   Did prophecie, that *Richmond* should be King,
   When *Richmond* was a little peeuish Boy.
   A King perhaps.
Buck.   May it please you to resolue me in my suit.
Rich.   Thou troublest me, I am not in the vaine.   *Exit.*
Buck.   And is it thus? repayes he my deepe seruice
   With such contempt?

The Quarto presents the incident in greater detail.

Buck.   What saies your highnes to my iust demand.
King.   As I remember, Henrie the sixt
   Did prophecie that Richmond should be king,

When Richmond was a little peeuish boy:
A king perhaps, perhaps.   *Buck.* My lord.
King. How chance the prophet could not at that time,
Haue told me I being by, that I should kill him.
Buck. My lord, your promise for the Earledom.
King. Richmond, when last I was at Exeter,
The Maior in curtesie showd me the Castle,
And called it Ruge-mount, at which name I started,
Because a Bard of Ireland told me once
I should not liue long after I saw Richmond.
Buck. My lord.
King. I, whats a clocke?
Buck. I am thus bold to put your grace in mind
Of what you promisd me.
King. Wel, but whats a clocke?
Buck. Upon the stroke of ten.
King. Well, let it strike.
Buck. Whie let it strike?
King. Because that like a Iacke thou keepst the stroke
Betwixt thy begging and my meditation,
I am not in the giuing vaine to day.
Buck. Whie then resolue me whether you wil or no?
King. Tut, tut, thou troublest me, I am not in the vain.
                                                    Exit.

Buck. Is it euen so, rewardst he my true seruice
With such deepe contempt, made I him king for this?

Daniel's explanation of this difference is on the
face of it unsatisfactory.

I can only account for the omission of this passage from
the Folio on the supposition that it never was in the original
draught of the play; that it was in fact, in theatrical par-
lance, a "bit of fat" inserted in the Q. version for the
benefit of the chief actor, when that version was put upon
the stage.[1]

---

[1] Introduction to *Richard III* (Griggs' Facsimile).

Daniel's conclusion that the "clock" passage must be an addition rests entirely on his general conclusion that the Folio has the original version, not on any particular characteristics in the passage itself; but his proof that the Folio is the original version relies in part on an argument which, applied to the passage now in question, leaves no doubt that at this particular point the Quarto text, not the Folio, is the earlier of the two. The confusion and contradiction in his argument become plain when the details are carefully considered.

Like Daniel, Schmidt[1] considered the Folio the original version and the "clock" passage as a later addition; in his endeavour to be more precise about the nature of this new material he completely exposes the weakness of their argument. He is not content to leave the question of the authorship of the addition in doubt, but insists that it was made by the actor playing the part. He pictures this individual revelling in the dramatic situation and the applause of the crowd, and prolonging the scene with unnecessary repetitions and additions. For one of these additions, introducing the prophecy of Richard's death, Holinshed, the main source for the play, must have been again consulted, and Schmidt remarks:

That the addition must therefore be by Shakespeare himself would be a hasty conclusion. For why should not his fellows have become familiar with Holinshed, if only because of the powerful drama that could not fail to interest them vitally? Why should they not have come by much of this in conversation with the poet? That they knew more of the history than actually stands in their parts is proved by the following circumstance. The Pursuivant

[1] *Shakespeare Jahrbuch*, No. 15, 1880.

with whom Hastings has a short conversation was also, according to Holinshed, called Hastings. Shakespeare made no use of this simple coincidence, and in the Folio there is no trace of it. To the actor however who played Hastings this fact was of the highest interest, and he dwelt on it with unnecessary emphasis.

This story from the green room can, however, be carried a little farther. Not only, it would seem, did the actor change his own part; he so infected the book-holder with this enthusiasm for historical detail that he in his turn altered the prompt book, and inserted a new stage direction. Unfortunately there is the more obvious explanation that what the "Pursuivant" passage actually proves is that, at this place, the Quarto preserves what stood in the original manuscript, and that the Folio gives a later version. There the Hastings passage stands:

Sta. But come, my Lord, let's away.

Enter a Pursuiuant.
Hast. Goe on before, Ile talke with this good fellow.

Exit Lord Stanley, and Catesby.
How now, Sirrha? how goes the World with thee?
Purs. The better, that your Lordship please to aske.

The Quarto reads:

But come my Lo: let us away.   *Enter Hastin.*
Hast. Go you before, Ile follow presently. (*a Purssuant.*
Hast. Well met Hastings, how goes the world with thee?
Pur. The better that it please your Lo: to aske.

Even to the reader this is confusing, and only a reference to the chronicle explains the apparently meaningless repetition; to a spectator it would be much more puzzling if it were not all over in a few seconds and forgotten. This is clearly the kind of

business that would eventually be altered by the
stage manager; if it had not stood in the original it
would never have been added. It is further just one
of these details from his sources, like the Bishop's
strawberries in Act III, sc. iv, which Shakespeare
often retained without any particular motive. In
discussing Act II, sc. iv, ll. 1–3 of the Folio Daniel
argued that since the Folio coincides with the
Chronicles, and the Quarto does not, this is "proof
positive that the Folio gives the first version of the
lines". In the "Pursuivant" passage the argument
applies even more strongly and is indeed irresistible;
to suppose the Hastings business a subsequent addition
is only possible in Schmidt's fairy tale.

The "clock" passage must obviously be considered
with the "Pursuivant" passage, and the argument
which proves the one Shakespeare's original applies
with equal force to the other. Nor is Daniel in his
attempt to establish the priority of the Folio entitled
to argue that agreement with Holinshed is a distinguishing mark of the first draft, and ignore this
evidence in the "clock" passage. This is a fatal
contradiction in his argument, unless he can show
that there are circumstances which make his proposition true in one place and not in the other; but
he has not proved that one reference to the original
source is due to the original author while another is
the work of a reviser; and merely to assume this is
to resort to guessing. The "clock" and "Pursuivant"
passages completely dispose of Daniel's argument that
the Quarto is a revised version of the Folio text.

Like the Quarto the Folio has passages peculiar to
itself which give some detail or other taken directly
from Holinshed and which there is no sufficient

reason for regarding as additions to the original text. The three lines (Act III, sc. v, ll. 103–5),

> Goe *Louell* with all speed to Doctor *Shaw*,
> Goe thou to Fryer *Peuker*, bid them both
> Meet me within this houre at Baynards Castle.

which refer to John Shaw and friar Penker, mentioned in Holinshed, are not found in the Quarto; nor does the line concerning Edward's contract with Lady Lucy (Act III, sc. vii, l. 5), also straight from the Chronicles, stand there. Neither text then, as we have it, is derived directly from the other. Both contain passages which stood in the original manuscript, but which are now found only in one or other of the printed versions; taken together these point to a version fuller and older than either.

When therefore Daniel and Schmidt, and we may add Delius,[1] insist that the Folio is the original version, they must now be understood to mean that the original version is more fully and accurately preserved in the Folio. Their assertion that editors should make the Folio the basis of their text may therefore still hold: their estimate of the help to be accepted from the Quarto requires revision.

Schmidt regarded the Quarto text as a shorthand report made in the theatre; the help it affords an editor must on this view be very occasional and fortuitous. When the players declaimed their parts correctly, and the reporter made no mistake, the Quarto may help to put right what the Folio printer has bungled; it has no further authority. This view may be dismissed at once. Schmidt took it for granted that all the Quartos issued before 1623 were stolen

---

[1] *Shakespeare Jahrbuch*, No. 7.

and surreptitious; these Quartos, he erroneously asserts, never claim to derive from the original copies, and as evidence of their origin he points to a few "errors of hearing" which they contain. Now that Heminge and Condell's words are better understood, and we know that compositors may change words which they are carrying in their heads to others of similar sound, there is no need to resort to such desperate opinions.

While Schmidt would reduce the value of the Quarto almost to nothing, Daniel insists on the importance of its readings; for although an editor, he admits, must depend chiefly on the Folio he will, he continues,

alter it in accordance with the Quarto in all places where it can be reasonably supposed that the variations of the Q. are the result of deliberate revision for the sake of correction or improvement.[1]

The phrase "for...correction or improvement" is necessary because the revision was intended in places to shorten and curtail parts; it is also required because, as Daniel recognized, this so-called revision frequently mangles the text. This by itself would be sufficient to make it doubtful whether Shakespeare was responsible for the alterations; and none of the passages with which Daniel supports his theory gives any warrant for supposing the text ever was *revised* in the sense he implies.

Daniel builds his argument on fifteen passages and these with his comments must now be examined;

[1] Introduction to *Richard III* (Griggs' Facsimile), by P. A. Daniel, p. xxi.

they will be taken in the order most convenient for analysis, Daniel's order being indicated in brackets.

(1) I, i, 138. *Folio.*

Now by S. *Iohn,* that Newes is bad indeed.

Quarto alters to Paul, the saint by whom Richard swears elsewhere. "Unless we suppose the *John* of F. to be a mere misprint, I do not see how we can avoid the conclusion that a deliberate change was made to *Paul* in the Q."

(2) I, ii, 19, 20. *Folio.*

Then I can wish to *Wolues, to* Spiders, Toades,
Or any creeping venom'd thing that liues.

"*Quarto* here has,—'to *adders,* Spiders', etc., an obvious correction."

(4) I, ii, 213. *Folio,* Crosbie *House*: *Quarto,* Crosbie *place.*

Since the name "Crosbie place" is found in the Chronicles, and since it is very improbable that "Wolues" stood in the author's manuscript, the view that the Quarto is in these instances a revision of the Folio must be replaced by the opposite conclusion that it is the Quarto that gives the unaltered readings, as it obviously does where it reads "Ludlow" for the Folio's "London" (Act II, sc. ii, ll. 142, 154).

(6) I, iv. *Folio* has Brackenbury and a keeper, while the *Quarto* only Brackenbury.

(9) II, iv. *Folio* has a Messenger to deliver the news at l. 37.

The *Quarto* gives it to Dorset.

(11) III, iv, v. *Folio* has Lovell and Ratcliff to execute Hastings.

The *Quarto* replaces them by Catesby, but retains the phrase "these our friends" (III, v, 54) which referred to Lovell and Ratcliff.

(13) v, i. *Folio* has a Sheriff at Buckingham's execution. The *Quarto* has Ratcliff.

(14) v, iii. *Folio* has a part for Surrey. The *Quarto* gives it to Catesby.

(15) v, iv. *Folio* in stage direction makes *Dorset* enter with Richmond, Brandon and Oxford. "In Q., Richmond enters only with 'Lordes, etc.' Malone supposes (Dorset not having been at the battle) that Dorset's name was put in the F. by the Players; on the contrary, I should suppose it to be struck out when the Q. was prepared."

These six instances are from stage directions, and it is the Quarto stage directions which provide the clue to the origin of the Quarto text. No one can dispute Daniel's conclusion that when the Quarto version was being made the original stage directions were altered so that the play could be performed by fewer actors; his evidence is conclusive. In the Folio (Act II, sc. iv) a messenger brings the news that Richard has contrived the murder of some of the Queen's kin: in the Quarto the news is conveyed by Dorset, but from the formal way he tells his mother of the deaths of her brother and of his own brother it is plain the messenger's part had only been assigned to the actor playing Dorset. Similarly in Act III, scenes iv and v, the duties of Lovell and Ratcliff had to be undertaken by Catesby; the abridger, however, by forgetting to excise the line in Act III, sc. v,

Catesby ouerlooke the wals.

presents us with the absurdity of Catesby on the stage and at the same time entering with the head of Hastings. The original stage directions have clearly been tampered with in the interests of stage economy, but the alterations are not part of a process that can be called *revision*.

Similar changes are noted by Dr Greg in his analysis of the Quarto of *Alcazar*. In Act II, sc. iii, of that play some lines have the prefix "Zareo"; as Zareo could have no business whatever in the scene Dr Greg concludes, "the name 'Zareo' here is a note indicating what player was available for the part". But the Quarto of *Alcazar* is not regarded as a revision of Peele's original version; and part of Dr Greg's judgment on *Alcazar* can undoubtedly be transferred to the Quarto of *Richard III*. It is a version cut down by the omission and reduction of speeches and by the elimination and doubling of parts for representation by a limited cast.

Even if this reduction were undertaken by Shakespeare himself it is doubtful how far the term "revision" could be applied to the new version; but there is ample evidence that this task was performed by another hand. Not content with noting that Dorset was to play the messenger in Act II, sc. iv, a difficulty that could easily have been covered up in actual representation, the abridger insists on emphasizing the incongruity of the situation by altering

> Heere comes a Messenger: What Newes?

to

> Here comes your sonne, Lo: M. Dorset.
> What newes Lo: Marques?

There is little doubt that the abridger was unaware of the historical inappropriateness of his transpositions either here or at the conclusion of Act III, sc. iv, and that, though someone of authority in the theatre, he was not the author himself.

Whoever was responsible for the version that contained these alterations in the stage directions and in the text no doubt made in addition the following changes, noted and commented on by Daniel.

(8) ii, iv, 1–3. *Folio.*

> Last night I heard they lay at Stony Stratford,
> And at Northampton they do rest to night:
> Tomorrow, or next day, they will be heere.

"Now this—an error as regards the conduct of the Play—curiously enough coincides with the Chronicles on which the play is founded: the young Prince on his way from Ludlow to London was actually taken back from Stony Stratford to Northampton. This seems to me proof positive that the F. gives the first version of the lines; but now comes the revision for the Q., and the reviser, recollecting that Stony Stratford is nearer to London than Northampton, gives us:

> Last night I heare they lay at Northampton
> At Stonistratford will they be to night,
> Tomorrow or next day they will be here.

This transposition of localities has the additional advantage of agreement with the *intention* of the author as expressed in the third line; and, whether it appear paradoxical or not, I should say that the slight sacrifice of rhythm involved in the change is another proof of the revision itself."

(3) i, ii, 180–2. *Folio.*

Nay do not pause: For I did kill King *Henrie*,
But 'twas thy Beauty that prouoked me.
Nay now dispatch: 'Twas I that stabb'd yong *Edward*,

"The Q. restores the historical order of these crimes, reading in the first line—'twas I that kild your husband'—and in the third—'kild King Henry'."

(5) i, iii, 333. *Folio.*

> To be reueng'd on *Riuers, Dorset, Grey.*

"For 'Dorset' the Q. substitutes 'Vaughan'; no doubt for the sufficient reason that he is associated in death with the other two."

(10) III, iii, 15–17. *Folio;* where Rivers, Vaughan and Grey are on their way to execution:

> *Grey.* Now *Margarets* Curse is falne upon our Heads,
> When shee exclaim'd on *Hastings,* you, and I,
> For standing by, when *Richard* stabb'd her Sonne.

"This is of course a direct reference to Margaret's curse in I, iii, 210–14; but Margaret had not there 'exclaimed on' *Grey,* but on Rivers, *Dorset* and Hastings. The Q. omits the second line of the passage quoted above, and perhaps the omission was due to some bungled attempt to conceal the discrepancy; if so, the reviser overlooked a second mis-statement in the line following the above—'then cursed she Buckingham'. Margaret did not then curse Buckingham."

None of these alterations is entitled to be called revision, and the next passage, where Daniel rightly considers the Quarto a mangled version of what we find in the Folio, is a curious example of a "reviser's" skill.

(12) IV, i. *Folio.*

> *Enter the Queene, Anne Duchesse of Gloucester, the Duchesse of Yorke, and Marquesse Dorset.*
>
> *Duch. Yorke.* Who meetes us heere?
> My Neece *Plantagenet,*
> Led in the hand of her kind Aunt of Gloster?
> Now, for my Life, shee's wandring to the Tower,

> On pure hearts loue, to greet the tender
> Prince.
> Daughter, well met.
>
> *Anne.* God giue your Graces both, a happie
> And a ioyfull time of day.
>
> *Qu.* As much to you, good Sister: whither away?

The Quarto has only—

*Enter Quee. mother, Duchesse of Yorke, Marques Dorset, at
one doore, Duchesse of Glocest. at another door.*

Duch. Who meets us heere, my neece Plantagenet?

Qu. Sister well met, whether awaie so fast?

"Now though no other indication of the presence of this
'Neece', either in the text or stage directions, is given in
F. or Q., I suppose all will admit that modern editors,
following Theobald, are right in defining her as Clarence's
young daughter; and the Duchess could no more be
supposed to address her daughter-in-law Anne as 'neece
Plantagenet' than the Queen could address this 'neece'
as sister; the presence therefore of *my neece Plantagenet* in
the Q. can only be accounted for as a remnant of the
passage *omitted* in the Q., and seems to me clear proof that
here the F. presents the original draught, and the Q. a
copy mangled in revision."

It is easy to give additional examples of the "reviser's"
carelessness. In Act iv, sc. iv, he transcribed the
lines (502–3),

> Sir *Edward Courtney*, and the haughtie Prelate,
> Bishop of Exeter,

as

> Sir William Courtney, and the haughtie Prelate,
> Bishop of Exceter,

and the lines (520–1),

> Sir *Thomas Louell*, and Lord Marquesse *Dorset*,
> 'Tis said, my Liege, in Yorkeshire are in Armes:

as

> Sir Thomas Louel, and Lord Marques Dorset,
> Tis said my liege, are up in armes.

The Chronicles support the Folio reading in both places.

It is already clear that an editor who wishes to restore what Shakespeare wrote ought not to follow, as Daniel recommends, the "revisions" in the Quarto text; he must adopt a contrary procedure, and accept the Quarto reading *only* where it preserves untouched those passages which he suspects that printers, editors, or stage managers have altered in the Folio.

Of the fifteen points enumerated by Daniel only the seventh remains for consideration. This deals with that curious passage in the Folio where Anthony Woodville, Lord Rivers, the Queen's brother, who was Lord Scales in right of his wife, is addressed by Richard as three separate persons, Lord Rivers, Lord Woodville and Lord Scales.

(7) ii, i, 66–8. *Folio.*

> Of you and you, Lord *Riuers* and of *Dorset,*
> That all without desert haue frownd on me:
> Of you Lord *Wooduill,* and Lord *Scales* of you.

Quarto.

> Of you Lo: Riuers, and Lord Gray of you,
> That all without desert haue frown'd on me.

The simplest explanation of this puzzle seems to be suggested by a peculiarity of the Folio stage directions. If the Quarto version was prepared for some occasion when the number of available actors must have been limited, the Folio version seems to have been played

by a company where there were enough and to spare.
In Act II, sc. i, at line 45 the Folio directs,

Enter Ratcliffe, and Gloster.

Ratcliffe has nothing to do except to swell the crowd
on the stage, and that he was a late-comer is further
indicated by the extension of the original line,

And in good time here comes the noble Duke.

preserved in the Quarto, into

And in good time,
Heere comes Sir *Richard Ratcliffe,* and the Duke.

Ratcliffe was put first because it was easier to fill out
the line that way, and because he was first mentioned
in the text he improperly stands before the Duke in
the stage direction. This desire to increase the number
on the stage may explain the presence of Woodville
as well as Rivers in the stage direction opening Act II,
sc. i, and of the addition of the line, "Of you Lord
Wooduill, and Lord *Scales* of you", where Rivers,
already two persons, is further divided into three.
That the play as printed in the Folio had undergone
some stage-editing in the long course of its successful
existence the "Pursuivant" passage provides conclusive evidence; the present puzzle may easily have
arisen in an editorial addition. The value of the
Quarto in this and certain other instances is that,
though a transcript made with a special end in view
and made on the whole with little care, it takes us
back beyond at least twenty-five years of supervision
by the stage manager, and that it has preserved not
only the "clock" passage but that admirable remark,
"O do not sweare my Lord of Buckingham", of the
witty and profound Richard.

But while the Quarto version may enable an
editor to get behind some at least of the stage
manager's work, it presents certain passages in what
can only be considered an unfinished state. The
playhouse copy, on the other hand, from which
Heminge and Condell had the corrections so laboriously transcribed to a copy of the sixth Quarto
(the copy for the Folio),[1] was possibly of the elaborate
kind used for the Folio versions of 2 and 3 *Henry VI*:
some of the new and more detailed directions in the
Folio of *Richard III* are in the style of the two
preceding plays,

> *Enter Duke of Glocester and Buckingham in armour*

of the Quarto becoming in the Folio,

> *Enter Richard, and Buckingham, in rotten Armour,*
> *maruellous ill-fauoured.*

This summarizes Holinshed's

himselfe with the duke of Buckingham stood harnessed in
old ill faring briganders, such as no man should weene,
that they would vouchsafe to haue put upon their backs,
except that some sudden necessitie had constreined them.

That more directions in this manner are not found
in the Folio may be due to the use of the Quarto
with its curter forms as a convenience in preparing
the copy for the printer in 1623. It is clear the
Quarto text was not abridged from a carefully
prepared manuscript, for it would not in these circumstances have been in the "chaotic condition" in
which, according to Daniel, we find it. If the Folio
manuscript was a finished and final version, it would

---

[1] As Daniel has proved, though Q 3 was used for Act III,
sc. i, ll. 17–165 and Act V, sc. iii, l. 50, to the end. See p. 212.

be natural for the Company to preserve it intact;
when circumstances made a hasty abridgment necessary they would have found it convenient to use the
author's foul papers, had they been available, which
could be scored and altered by the abridger. Copy of
this nature would explain some of the worst examples
of "revision" already noted in the Quarto; it would
also account for certain repetitions in that text
pointed out by Daniel.

At Act I, sc. iv, ll. 251–3, Clarence tells the
murderers how he parted from Gloucester,

Folio.
> It cannot be, for he bewept my Fortune,
> And hugg'd me in his armes, and swore with sobs,
> That he would labour my deliuery.

Quarto.
> It cannot be, for when I parted with him,
> He hugd me in his armes,

The phrase, "hugd me in his arme", also occurs
in the Quarto in what Daniel calls the "extraordinary
verses" at Act II, sc. ii, ll. 23–4.

> And when he tould me so, he wept,
> And hugd me in his arme, and kindly kist my cheeke,

The Folio is slightly different,

> And when my Unckle told me so, he wept,
> And pittied me, and kindly kist my cheeke.

Since Daniel regarded the Folio as the original version,
he had to suppose that Shakespeare wished to transfer
the phrase "hugg'd me in his armes" from Clarence's
story to that of his son, but failed to do so clearly,
hence confusion and repetition. It is, however, quite
as probable that Shakespeare discovered he had used

the phrase twice and deleted the second instance; the Quarto shows a provisional alteration made final in the Folio. Since the evidence as a whole is against the Quarto being a revised text this view of the change is the more likely; the slight evidence given by the Chronicle also points this way. Holinshed tells of Richard's dissimulation towards the youthful Duke of York, and how "the protector tooke him in his arms and kissed him". It would not be surprising if Shakespeare transferred this phrase to his dealings with Clarence's son, and he would hardly have cancelled it in that context unless he had found himself using it in a previous place. Similarly the Quarto repetition,

    III, i, 188–9.

Glo. Shall we heare from you Catesby ere we sleepe?
Cat. You shall my Lord.

    IV, ii, 84–5.

King. Shal we heare from thee *Tirrel* ere we sleepe?
Tir. Ye shall my lord.

is removed in the Folio by the omission of the second passage. These repetitions are only further indications that the Quarto gives in places Shakespeare's un-revised draft of the play.

Though it is possible to disagree about the details of the relationship between Folio and Quarto, it is clear how unnecessary is the haste with which the differences between the Quarto and the Folio are explained as the work of various authors. This extreme assumption can only be justified when the lesser possibilities have proved inadequate. But the differences between the Quarto and Folio texts of *Richard III* do not call for such arbitrary treatment and can very well be accommodated to the theory that the Folio preserves, though not completely, the carefully prepared prompt copy long in the possession of the Company, and that the Quarto is an abridgment made at an early period for a special purpose, possibly from Shakespeare's own rough draft. The divergencies between the Quarto and Folio texts of *Richard III* and the differences between 2 and 3 *Henry VI* and their respective Quartos are therefore equally worthless as proof that the plays are from several hands.

It would indeed have been a remarkable coincidence if the Marlowe, Peele, Greene theory invented by Malone, quite unnecessarily, as has been shown, to explain the textual difficulties of 2 and 3 *Henry VI* should have solved the further problem of *Richard III*. Malone himself protested against the extended use of this formula which was rapidly becoming a favourite critical weapon even in his own day.

In consequence of the publication of the Dissertation on the Three Parts of King Henry the Sixth, in which I endeavoured to shew that these plays were formed on dramas written by more ancient poets than Shakespeare, a strange and whimsical fancy seems to have been entertained by various critics, that this notion is applicable to several other of our author's plays. (Boswell's *Malone*, iv, 148.)

His judgments, he thought, in contrast to these fancies rested on firm textual ground. But as long as *Richard III* seemed to provide equally secure textual footing there was no reason why Malone's arguments should not have been extended to it: once, however, it is clear that no textual support exists for this argument in 2 and 3 *Henry VI* themselves, let alone in *Richard III*, it becomes necessary to reject the

exaggerated significance that has been attached to
minor bibliographical features in the texts. Subsequent critics have shown remarkable ingenuity in
following up clues which lead to conclusions similar
to Malone's; and no one has proved apter in this
detective work than Fleay. On passing to 1 *Henry VI*
it will be necessary to demonstrate how extravagant
are the conclusions he draws from his evidence: before leaving the field clear in *Richard III* for literary
critics it is necessary to warn them that in this plot
also Fleay has sown the tares of rash conjecture.

He first laid emphasis on the Derby-Stanley
variation. Lord Stanley, who was not made Earl of
Derby till the time of Henry VII, is throughout the
first two acts of *Richard III* referred to as Derby
both in the text and in the stage directions. From
Act III, sc. i, however, the Folio always calls him
Stanley in the text though occasionally Derby in
stage directions, while the Quarto, which in these
scenes frequently has Stanley both in the text and
stage directions, has Derby not only in stage directions
but, in contrast to the Folio, in the text itself. It has
been argued that when the text of *Richard III* was
revised for the Quarto version this change was made
by a new author whose hand can be traced from
Act III; but it has been shown that the Quarto is not
a revised version, and even this Derby-Stanley variation gives no support to the suggestion. Since the
so-called revised text actually has Derby where the
Folio has Stanley it proves if anything the opposite
of what is claimed, and Fleay himself argued that it
showed "a progressive correction in which Q.
precedes F." Fleay, however, went on to claim that
this and similar variations prove *Richard III* the

work of more than one author. But there is no well-established body of bibliographical evidence to support the view that these variants are necessarily due to several original hands, and alternative explanations readily present themselves; Fleay's statement is the merest guess, and can have no weight whatever against the contemporary evidence which attributes *Richard III* to Shakespeare. Criticism of 1 *Henry VI*, in the absence of a Quarto text, tends to degenerate into wild conjecture about similar details, and here there is sufficient scope for Fleay to entangle himself in his own ingenuity.

(iii) 1 *Henry VI*

Fleay began his examination of 1 *Henry VI* by looking for a method that would enable him to discriminate the various hands he took for granted in its composition. He first separated the play into five groups of scenes distinguished by their historical time and place: the scenes of Group A have a time limit 1422–6 and are all laid in London; Group B contains only events that happened between 1427 and 1430; for Group C the time is 1435, the place Rouen; Group D is made up of the Joan of Arc story of 1430–1 and the Margaret match of 1443. There is finally the group dealing with Talbot's last fight near Bordeaux in 1452; this belongs chronologically to the next play, and Fleay regarded it as Shakespeare's addition to the "old" play. The other groups he considered as each the work of a different author.

The idea that groups of scenes dealing with events that lie far apart in history can only have been brought together in an historical play by different hands is on the face of it absurd: it is obvious that the drawing together of the various threads of diverse happenings is one of the most characteristic features of Shakespeare's histories. These are not history but drama, and all the dramatic liberties with historical material that are found in 1 *Henry VI* can be paralleled in their kind in Shakespeare's other plays. It would be as sensible to suggest that *Macbeth* must be by two hands because it brings together material from two reigns, King Duncan's and King Duff's, as to suppose that Fleay's historical division of 1 *Henry VI* has any bearing on the authorship.

This mode of division by itself could have no authority, but Fleay claimed that it was supported by more remarkable differences: each group was separated from the other not merely by historical content but by an individual way of spelling proper names. This, if Fleay were correct, would be an invaluable instrument for distinguishing the authors, and Professor Allison Gaw has rightly emphasized the point in his recent study of 1 *Henry VI*.

One of the chief bases for Fleay's division, that of the spelling of certain proper names, is, as here [in Professor Gaw's study] employed, more or less mechanical; but for that reason it is all the more valuable, both as in general the result of the automatic operation of fixed spelling habits in the writer, and as not liable to subjective errors of interpretation due to the personal equation of the investigator. Although largely ignored by commentators since Fleay's discovery of them, these points must be accorded the consideration they deserve.[1]

[1] *The Origin and Development of* 1 *Henry VI*, by Allison Gaw, p. 68.

Unfortunately Professor Gaw himself in his very exhaustive study has not considered Fleay's claim with sufficient attention.

Fleay's historical groups and their corresponding spellings may be tabulated in this way:

A (I, i, iii;   *Gloster Roän*   *Reynold*
  II, v; III, i)
B (I, ii, iii, iv, v, *Gloucester* or *Ioane Puzel Burgundy Reignier*
  vi; II, i, ii, iii; *Glocester*   (or -*eir*)
  III, iv; IV, i)
C (III, ii, iii)   *Roan Ioane Pucell Burgonie*

D (v, ii–v)   *Gloucester* or *Ione   Pucell Burgundy Reignier*
                 Glocester

A brief examination, however, of these variations shows that the evidence is not so compact as the table suggests.

In 1 *Henry VI, Gloucester* is spelt in three ways which are distributed as follows:

Act I, sc. i.   *Gloster*; 2 in text, 2 in stage directions.
                 Glost., before speeches 6.
    sc. iii.   *Gloster*; 7 in text, 3 in stage directions.
                 Glost., before speeches 14.
Act II, sc. iv. *Gloucester*; 1 in text.
Act III, sc. i. *Gloster*; 7 in text, 2 in stage directions.
                 Glost., before speeches 11.
                 Glocester; 1 in text.
    sc. iv.   *Gloucester*; 1 in text, 1 in stage direction.
Act IV, sc. i.   *Glocester*; 1 in stage direction.
Act V, sc. i.   *Gloster*; 1 in text.
                 Glocester; 1 in stage direction.
    sc. v.   *Glocester*; 2 in stage directions.
                 Gloucester; 1 before a speech.

Up to and including Act III, sc. i, the spelling is *Gloster* with two exceptions; after that *Gloster* is the exception. It is also from Act III, sc. ii, that the

spelling *Pucell* for earlier *Puzel* makes its appearance,
and *Burgonie* for *Burgundy; Ioane*, however, is retained as before. With Act IV the spelling *Burgundy*
is restored, and in Act V *Ioane* becomes *Ione*. To
suppose, however, that these variations are the result
of the automatic operation of fixed spelling habits in
Marlowe, Greene, Peele, or whoever are named as
the various authors, is the assumption that requires
consideration.

It is impossible here to examine completely the
Folio spelling of *Gloucester*. The forms it assumes in
the word *Gloucestershire* may serve as a sample. The
Folio and Quarto spellings of the eight examples
found in the Concordance are shown in this list.

		Folio	Quartos
M. W. W.	III, iv, 44	*Glocestershire*	*Glostershire*
	V, v, 191	*Glostershire*	—
Richard II	II, iii, 3	*Gloustershire*	*Glocestershire*
	V, vi, 3	*Gloucestershire*	*Gloucestershire*
1 *Henry IV*	I, iii, 243	*Gloustershire*	*Glocestershire*
	III, ii, 176	*Glocestershire*	*Glocestershire*
2 *Henry IV*	IV, iii, 88	*Gloucestershire*	*Glostershire*
	IV, iii, 138	*Gloucestershire*	*Glostershire*

If variation is sought within narrower limits *Lear*,
Act III, sc. vii, shows *Gloucester* in three forms. The
spellings in Q 1 and Q 2 are added for completeness.

Folio	Q 1	Q 2
Glouster	*Gloster*	*Glocester*
Glouster	*Gloster*	*Glocester*
Glouster	*Gloster*	*Glocester*
Gloster	*Gloster*	*Glocester*
Gloucester	*Gloster*	*Glocester*

Here Q 2, which is a reprint of Q 1, changes *Gloster*
to *Glocester*, while in the Quartos of *Richard III* the

later editions frequently change *Glocester* to *Gloster*.
But uniformity and irregularity in spelling this name
alternate in a quite unpredictable manner. *Burgundy*
also varies in *Henry V* as well as in 1 *Henry VI*: in
the closing scene of the former history it occurs four
times, each time with a different spelling, *Bourgongne*,
Burgogne, *Burgonie*, *Burgundy*; to these four forms
may be added a fifth from Act IV, sc. viii, l. 102,
Burgundie. In *Henry V* the spellings *Gloster* and
Gloucester can be seen in consecutive lines. *Joan*
does not occur frequently in any of the Folio plays
except 1 *Henry VI*, but on its few appearances some
plays spell *Ione*, others *Ioane*. While therefore it is
the business of the bibliographer to believe with
Fluellen that "there is occasions and causes why and
wherefore in all things," and therefore in spelling, he
may be asked to consider the habits of the Folio
compositors before he regards the Folio as recording
the automatic operation of fixed spelling habits; he
may also be asked to reflect on Shakespeare's own
practice before he comes to any conclusion.

In 1 *Henry VI*, Act I, sc. iii, the spelling *Gloster*
occurs seven times in the text, but on three occasions
the word has to be pronounced as three syllables; the
original spelling must have been *Glocester* or *Gloucester*. Presumably this is why Fleay assigns the
scene to B, who is supposed to spell *Glocester*, as well
as to A. But the most cursory search shows that there
is no ground whatever for supposing that Shakespeare did not vary the pronunciation to suit himself.
In the last scene of 1 *Henry IV*, *Worcester* will be
found used as a word both of two and of three
syllables; and while *Worcester* is the normal spelling
Worster is also found in Act v, sc. i, of the same play.

Fleay's distinction therefore in 1 *Henry VI* between Rouen in Act 1, sc. i, where it is two syllables, and elsewhere, where it can be regarded as one, is equally without significance. Finally the form *Reynold*, supposed to be characteristic of A, is only found once, and, like *Reignard* of Act IV, sc. iv, is an obvious misprint, or error in reading the *Reigneir* of the manuscript. That the mistake was easily made the spelling *Reynard* at the conclusion of 3 *Henry VI* and *Raynard* in a transcribed passage in *The Contention* afford additional evidence.[1] Shakespeare's practice may also have been affected by the spelling differences in the various chronicles before him.

It is a commonly received idea in these discussions on authorship that Shakespeare only made use of one chronicle, Holinshed's, and that the presence of phrases and material from other chronicles is evidence of the work of other men. This was first circulated by Malone, who tried to show that *The Contention*

[1] All that is of value in this argument against Fleay from the variations in the spelling of proper names elsewhere in the Folio has been anticipated by Mr H. T. Price in the *Beiblatt zur Anglia*, April 1928; it was worked out, however, as it stands here quite independently of Mr Price, at the close of 1927. I am glad to find myself in agreement with so acute a critic. Mr Price also disposes of another of Professor Gaw's arguments.

"Professor Gaw thinks that the numerous self contradictory passages in the play prove the presence of work by several hands. The correspondence columns of English periodicals, however, are continually bringing to light instances of similar contradictions in undoubted one man works. 'Affable Hawk' in the *New Statesman* is finding such contradictions in the Sherlock Holmes series that if they occurred in an English play they would be acclaimed an absolute proof of composite authorship."

For similar contradictions in Bunyan see *Essays in Satire*, by Father Knox.

and *Richard Duke of York* were based on Halle while
the "revision" by Shakespeare was dependent on
Holinshed. But this purely artificial distinction breaks
down even if we accept the Quartos, for what they
are not, as early versions of 2 and 3 *Henry VI*. The
molehill on which York has to stand before his
murder in *Richard Duke of York*, as well as in
3 *Henry VI*, is not found in Halle but in Holinshed;
the Quarto versions, even if they were Shakespeare's
originals, would therefore have to be regarded as in
part from Holinshed; and some of Shakespeare's
corrections as derived from Halle. When, however,
the true nature of the Quartos is admitted, Malone's
idea that Shakespeare used Holinshed to the exclusion
of the other chroniclers is found to rest on one piece
of positive evidence: there are a few mistakes in
Shakespeare's historical matter that can be traced to
Holinshed. To suppose that this is proof that he never
consulted other chronicles is not only to go further
than the evidence will stretch, but to take for granted
what has yet to be proved, that the phrases from Halle,
Grafton, Fabyan, and others, which are found in his
works, are the insertions of other hands.

The variation therefore between *Puzel* of the
earlier scenes of 1 *Henry VI* and *Pucell* of the second
part may well be due to Shakespeare himself. He had
Puzel before him in Grafton and Halle, and *Pusell* in
Holinshed.

It is now safe to say that the variety in the spelling
of the proper names of the play has no connection
whatever with the historical divisions Fleay discovered in it, and that any attempt to employ these
various spellings in the mechanical way suggested
by Fleay and so strongly approved of by Professor

Allison Gaw can only be regarded as misdirected ingenuity.

Nor need this conclusion be modified because what is called the literary evidence for the authorship supports in a very astonishing way the method of division here set aside. Literary evidence might well be regarded as beyond the scope of a merely textual study of the plays, but it is in this instance of a peculiar kind. Before it can be considered, however, it is necessary to dispose of another of Fleay's arguments suggested by the irregularity of the act and scene division of the Folio text.

Acts I and II are correctly marked, but except for the heading *Scœna Prima* that accompanies *Actus Primus* and *Secundus* there are no indications of scene division. Act III is divided into four scenes, but after the heading *Actus Quartus. Scena Prima.* several scenes intervene (the Talbot scenes, and the subsidiary scenes with York and Somerset which explain the defeat and death of Talbot) before the heading *Scena secunda* makes its appearance; then follow *Scœna Tertia* and another two unmarked scenes (the interview between Suffolk and Margaret, and the trial of Joan and surrender of the French); there is finally a concluding scene headed *Actus Quintus*. Fleay at once turned to the explanation with which he solved all difficulties: these irregularities were due to the faulty joining of the work of various authors. The scenes of Act IV that are not numbered at all were, he considered, an interpolation by Shakespeare; but he never asked himself how what is headed scene two could ever have followed scene one without the intervention of the very episodes which he regarded as additional and superfluous matter. They are, how-

ever, the very substance and core of the original plot.
The explanation which Professor Pollard and his
bibliographical class at King's College, London, first
proposed is different and clearly correct. This *scene ii*
is scene ii not of Act IV but of Act V, and the heading
before the concluding scene *Actus Quintus* is an error
for *Scena Quinta*. There is a similar error in *King
John* where *Actus Secundus* stands for *Scena Secunda*.
If, however, we count from what may now be regarded as scene ii of Act V we find that after

> *Scene ii*—between the King, Gloucester and
>   Winchester,
> *Scene iii*—the capture of Joan,
> *Scene (unnumbered)*—Suffolk and Margaret,
> *Scene (unnumbered)*—sentence of Joan and sur-
>   render of the French,

the final scene should be scene vi, not scene v. But
if we regard the scene between Suffolk and Margaret
as an addition, then the last appearance of Joan and
the French surrender would have been numbered iv,
so that another addition at the end could easily have
been numbered v in error, merely from a reference to
this preceding scene. The two scenes that deal with
the Margaret match can be regarded as interpolations,
because unlike the Talbot scenes they have nothing
to do with the plot and are clearly additions to link
I *Henry VI* to 2 *Henry VI*. But that these links are
not by the author of the play as a whole does not
follow in any way from the bibliographical evidence.
That they are the work of the author of the other
scenes can be taken for granted till it is shown that
they are not.

It is more difficult to explain how the act and

scene numberings came to be omitted elsewhere, but there are similar omissions in other Folio versions where interpolation cannot be given as the explanation. It need not be resorted to here. Till the whole question of the act and scene division of Shakespeare's plays is better understood and an acceptable explanation of the omission of division in the Quartos propounded, it is unsafe to guess about particular instances. One point, however, seems certain, that, although the Quartos, with the exception of *Othello* (1622) and *Romeo and Juliet* (1597), are not divided, Shakespeare made his plays in five acts. It has been suggested that Shakespeare followed the older native tradition while Ben Jonson held after classical precedent; but Shakespeare's early plays are much nearer Plautus and Seneca than anything of Jonson's. Shakespeare early studied drama in the works of the Latin and Italian dramatists; they were the models for the schoolmasters and their schools. To what the schoolmasters of one generation taught, the men of genius of the next gave form and expression; and for once—for although Milton kept a school Phillips informs us he only received "the sons of some gentlemen that were his intimate friends"—the schoolmaster and the man of genius were the same person. To ignore the influence of Shakespeare's early reading is to recognize that his schoolmastering had not made him a pedagogue, but it is to be deceived by the modesty of his art. Marlowe, who can hardly be supposed to follow native tradition rather than classical example, has one play, *Edward II*, which was printed in Quarto without indication of acts or scenes. *Tamburlaine* on the other hand is divided into the regulation five acts. *Edward II* was played by, and presumably written for, Pembroke's men, the Company who at one time possessed the copies of 2 and 3 *Henry VI* printed without division in the Folio. We cannot suppose, however, that the difference between *Tamburlaine* and *Edward II* is due to one theatre having a different practice from another; some may have had much music, others little, but the five acts provided the opportunity for music and were not first invented to suit the musicians. Even if the actors had ignored the act divisions the author would still have found them a convenient scaffolding for his work, as he did no doubt in his earlier composition. The absence of acts and scenes from the printed text of *Edward II* does not prove they had no place in the dramatist's conception of that play; their absence therefore from Shakespeare Quartos is no proof that Shakespeare's practice in this matter was different from that of Marlowe. The omission of scene headings in 1 *Henry VI* is part of a larger problem, still unsolved, but has no necessary connection with the authorship of that work.[1]

The disintegration of the play must therefore depend on the literary evidence. Hart has had the honour of being called the best of the modern editors of 1 *Henry VI*; his method and conclusions may therefore be examined with no injustice to those who claim this play as the work of other men than Shakespeare. He explains in his preface[2] that his views arose from a study of the literary parallels between this play and others, and that a consideration of these

[1] See *Review of English Studies*, July 1926, October 1927, for the views of Sir Mark Hunter and Professor Dover Wilson on "Act- and Scene-Division in Shakespeare."

[2] Arden edition.

parallels is the test of his theories. He begins his analysis as follows:

Act i.

   i, i, 23. *planets of mishap.* Borne underneath the Planet of mishap (*Alphonsus,* Grosart, xiii, 391).
   i, i, 67. *cause him once more yield the ghost.* Without *to.* Twice again in *Henry VIII.* Uncommon in Elizabethan writers, "Whose fathers he causd murthered in these warres" (George-a-Greene). Greene wrote a sketch of this scene, but it is mainly by Shakespeare rewritten.

This is only one end of the web, but Dr Johnson's assurance that where one picks up pack-thread it is useless to look for embroidery may excuse further quotation. Professor Gaw adopts a similar method to show that the same scene is the work of Marlowe. Most of his parallels are with *The Contention* or *Richard Duke of York* and are therefore useless as clues to authorship; of the others the following are fair samples:

   (*a*) *Jew of Malta,* 758.
Instead of gold,
We'le send thee bullets wrapped in smoake and fire.
   1 *Henry VI,* i, i, 46.
    In stead of Gold, wee'le offer up our Armes.
   (*b*) *Tamburlaine,* 4021.
    Haling him headlong to the lowest hell.
   1 *Henry VI,* i, i, 149.
    Ile hale the Dolphin headlong from his Throne.

To those who find any evidential value in such parallels may be left the difficult decision between Greene and Marlowe.

   There remains the question whether Shakespeare's 1 *Henry VI* is the same play as that mentioned in

Henslowe's *Diary*. The latter was performed by Lord
Strange's men at the Rose theatre shortly before the
London Companies were driven into the provinces
by the closing of the theatres in 1592. Shakespeare
became a member of this Company, now called the
Chamberlain's Company, after their return to
London in the summer of 1594; but there is no
evidence that he wrote anything for them before
1594, although their repertory is known in considerable detail. This important negative evidence
agrees with the positive indications that he was a
member of Pembroke's Company before that Company went on tour. He cannot very well then be
considered the author of the play put on at the Rose
for the first time on 3 March 1592 by Strange's men;
but as the Company that played this play was later
joined by Shakespeare, it has been suggested that he
added the two short scenes between Margaret and
Suffolk, which are clearly interpolations, to link it
to his own plays on the reign of *Henry VI*. It now
became the first part of a trilogy and was for this
reason included in his collected works, although he
had only added a few lines to it. Shakespeare, on this
view, must have written the additions which connect this play with his own some time after 1594
when he joined his new Company.

But there is at least some evidence that what is
printed in the First Folio as 1 *Henry VI* was in the
repertory of Pembroke's men in 1593, and that what
are clearly the latest additions to the play, the
Margaret-Suffolk scenes, existed as early as August
of that year. If this were admitted, it would no longer
be possible to identify 1 *Henry VI* with the play
performed at the Rose in 1592, for one must have

belonged to Strange's or the Admiral's men and the other to Pembroke's; and there is no evidence of Pembroke's Company selling their plays to Henslowe or to Strange's men till they came back to London in the summer of 1593 after a disastrous tour in the provinces. The plausible suggestion that Shakespeare linked a Strange play to his own earlier Pembroke plays would therefore be disproved, for it would follow that not only was the 1 *Henry VI* of the Folio *not* a Strange play, but that the links which are supposed to point to that Company's play being bound to Shakespeare's existed before Shakespeare and his plays were associated with them.

The Bad Quartos of 2 and 3 *Henry VI* put together by some players in Pembroke's Company contain passages from other plays with which they were familiar as well as from those they were trying to reproduce. They drew freely on *Edward II*, which is described in the Quarto of 1594 as acted by Pembroke's servants. Echoes from older plays like *Tamburlaine* or *The Spanish Tragedy*, even although these were in the possession of other Companies, are not surprising since these plays were widely known. What we would not expect would be interpolations from the latest productions of other Companies. When therefore they confuse a passage in 2 *Henry VI* with that from a similar situation in 1 *Henry VI*, or transfer an expression from the latter to *The Contention* in their struggle to reconstruct the text of 2 *Henry VI*, it is fair to assume they are drawing on another play in their repertory. In *The Contention* York, expounding his pedigree, refers to

The right and title of the house of Yorke,
To Englands Crowne by liniall desent.

These lines the reporter put together from various

sources which included 1 *Henry VI*, Act III, sc. i,
ll. 165–6,

> That doth belong unto the House of *Yorke*,
> From whence you spring, by Lineall Descent.

Again, in the opening scene, where Henry is receiving his bride from Suffolk's hands, he speaks of
his "perplexed soule". Naturally no such phrase
stands at this point in 2 *Henry VI*, and the reporter
is clearly recalling the earlier scene at the close of
1 *Henry VI*. There the King, though the Protector
reminds him he is breaking his vow to another lady,
allows Suffolk to persuade him to send for Margaret;
in this difficult situation he urges Suffolk to carry
through his commission quickly—

> Be gone I say, for till you do returne,
> I rest perplexed with a thousand Cares.

The repetition of *perplexed* when Henry at last has
his wish might convict the reporter of cynicism or
misogyny did we not know that in his troubles he
was glad to lay hold of any tag without overmuch
reflection on its propriety. Since this transference is
from the very latest addition to 1 *Henry VI*, it is
impossible to regard the last scene of that play as
added by Shakespeare after he joined the Chamberlain's Company; it already stood there in 1593 when
1 *Henry VI* was familiar to Pembroke's men, presumably because it was then in their repertory.

Some evidence can thus be brought against the
identification of Shakespeare's 1 *Henry VI* and the
Henry VI in Henslowe's *Diary*. And there is no
objection to the view that there were several plays
on this reign by different authors: there were at least
two plays about Richard III, and the *Richard II*
Forman saw at the Globe was not Shakespeare's. If

we did not know more about Shakespeare's doings in 1602 than in 1592, it would be difficult to avoid identifying certain of his later plays with others on similar subjects entered in Henslowe's *Diary*; confusion over *Troilus and Cressida* would be inevitable, and it might be possible to represent *Henry IV* as a revision of *The Life of Sir John Oldcastle* were this Quarto also missing. This admitted, the entry in Henslowe's *Diary* need not refer to the 1 *Henry VI* of the Folio, and the last shred of external evidence that 1 *Henry VI* is not by Shakespeare disappears. Nashe's encomium therefore may be taken as a reference to Shakespeare's play or to that performed at the Rose; since we know that Shakespeare's play introduces Talbot, and we know nothing of the other, we may venture to think Nashe referred to the play by Shakespeare.

The theory which has been examined at length in these pages, that Marlowe, Greene, Peele, or some other of Shakespeare's contemporaries, were the authors of the greater part of the York and Lancaster plays in the Folio, has been shown, it is hoped, to have originated in misunderstanding and error, and to have been extended on the most unsatisfactory pretexts. Those, however, who refuse to accept the plays as Shakespeare's, although they have yet to advance a sound argument for their opinion, rely perhaps on more than reason. Like Falstaff, they may possess an instinct which would warn them of the presence of the true Prince; however dark and confused the textual situation they know their Shakespeare. We must all sympathize with the attitude of the Knight; but Falstaff is a dangerous example; and the student who lacks some of this instinct must trust to Heminge and Condell.

V. THE FIRST PERIOD

THE interpretation of the earliest references to
the acting or publication of the plays of this
period in Shakespeare's work has almost in-
variably been based on the assumption that *The
Contention, Richard Duke of York* and *The Taming of
a Shrew* were composed before the corresponding
plays in the Folio of 1623, and on the further
assumption that the "old" plays were the work of
Marlowe, Greene, Peele, Lodge, Kyd, or Nashe, and
that Shakespeare's first period as a dramatist, when
as Dowden put it he was "in the workshop", was
spent in revising the work of these men. But the
Quartos of the three "old" plays give no more than
pirated versions of Shakespeare's texts, and there
remains no certain evidence that Shakespeare began
by revising the work of others; there is nothing which
entitles commentators to accommodate the information concerning Shakespeare in Henslowe's *Diary*, the
Stationers' Register and other contemporary documents to their revising theory. The many convenient
assumptions which they have found necessary for the
systematic presentation of this material not merely
ignore the testimony of Heminge and Condell, of
Meres and Greene, but misinterpret the textual
evidence at our disposal in *The Contention, Richard
Duke of York*, and *a Shrew*. Some of these assumptions can now be put aside at once as erroneous.

The first to go must be the commonly received
opinion that Shakespeare did not begin to write for

the stage till about 1591. "We may start", says Sir Arthur Quiller-Couch, "from the year 1591 and take the ensuing twenty as the period covering Shakespeare's career as a dramatist." But Malone, who first made this suggestion, recognized that it was only a guess: "If I were to indulge a conjecture", he says, "I should name the year 1591, as the era when our author commenced a writer for the stage", although, as he himself adds, Shakespeare was by this time twenty-seven years old. The reasons for his conjecture are particularly unconvincing: Shakespeare's name is not found in Webbe's *Discourse of English Poetry* (1586), nor in Puttenham's *Art of English Poesy* (1589), nor in Sir John Harington's *Apologie for Poetrie* prefixed to his version of the *Orlando Furioso* (1591), and Malone concluded he could not have written anything for the stage by those dates. Long ago, however, Knight pointed out that these works were even in their own day completely out of date in their references to the theatre; they make no mention of Marlowe, Greene, Peele or Kyd, and no one will contend that these dramatists did not begin their work before 1591; why should the omission of Shakespeare's name be any more significant? And the final piece of evidence which shows that Malone had not considered the matter with sufficient care is his statement,

Sir Philip Sidney, in his Defence of Poesie, speaks at some length of the low state of dramatick literature at the time he composed this treatise; but has not the slightest allusion to Shakespeare, whose plays, had they then appeared, would doubtless have rescued the English stage from the contempt which is thrown upon it by this accomplished writer.

Knight's reply that Sir Philip Sidney was killed at Zutphen in 1586, and that *An Apologie for Poetrie* was written some years before, though not published till 1595, needs no elaboration. Malone's conjecture arose from the confusion caused by his interpretation of Greene's words against "the upstart Crow", and became a necessary corollary to his proposition about *The Contention* and *Richard Duke of York.*

Another view that has grown up under the protection of Malone's maintains that Shakespeare had written nothing as a whole before 1593, the date of *Venus and Adonis*, and relies on the statement in the dedicatory epistle to the poem that it was "the first heire" of his invention. This, however, need mean no more than the first of his published works, and we know from Chettle that at the time of Greene's attack Shakespeare was already known for "his facetious grace in writing"; and indeed this was what called forth Greene's jealous invective, not any patching of his plays. Mr Robertson's interpretation of the metaphorical phrase must remain merely arbitrary, unless he can re-establish Malone's interpretation of Greene's words and his view of *The Contention* and *Richard Duke of York.* The very title page of *Venus and Adonis* suggests that Shakespeare was already a poet of considerable reputation. In the epistle to Southampton he speaks of his powers with that noble modesty, which, as Lamb has said, we can neither imitate nor appreciate; but what there was yet to know we can learn from the Latin motto,

> Vilia miretur vulgus: mihi flavus Apollo
> Pocula Castalia plena ministret aqua.

That his demerits could speak unbonneted to as

proud a fortune as this that he had reached was not a confidence to an unknowing world unacquainted with his history. But though this is dismissed as fanciful the external evidence of his previous activity cannot be explained away.

The central fact round which the fragmentary information of Shakespeare's early career in London must be arranged is the Plague of 1592–3. This and other disturbances drove the London Companies into the provinces in 1592, and when they settled down again in town in the spring and summer of 1594 there are important changes to record. It is a safe conjecture, however, that the plays they took into the provinces in 1592 they brought back again without additions to their number: a company on tour would have no need or desire to commission new work. And it is even safer to conjecture that during these months Shakespeare at least was not continuously employed in writing for the stage, as his *Venus and Adonis* and *Lucrece* appeared in 1593 and 1594. Those of his plays, therefore, which are known to have been played or published immediately after the return of the leading Companies, or performed during the brief visits of Sussex's and the Queen's men to the Rose in January and April,[1] may be considered as having been composed by Shakespeare before the Plague and the departure of the Companies.

The plays of Shakespeare which may on these grounds be dated before midsummer 1592 are: *The Comedy of Errors*,[2] *The Taming of the Shrew*,[3] *Titus*

[1] *Henslowe's Diary*, ed. Dr W. W. Greg, I, 16–17.
[2] Acted at Gray's Inn, December 1594.
[3] Bad Quarto entered Stationers' Register, May 1594; Shakespeare's play acted at Newington Butts, June 1594.

Andronicus,[1] 2[2] and 3[3] *Henry VI*, to which may be added 1 *Henry VI*,[4] and possibly an early version of *Hamlet*.[5] This reasonable assumption is supported by further evidence that can be produced for the date of each of these works.

The three Quarto title pages that enable us to assign *The Taming of the Shrew*, *Titus Andronicus*, 2 and 3 *Henry VI* to Pembroke's Company leave no doubt that these were written before the tour which ended so disastrously for that Company about August 1593; there are in addition early references to 3 *Henry VI*,[6] 1 *Henry VI*[7] and *Hamlet*[8] by Greene and Nashe.

But there are references which carry back certain plays to a much earlier date. Malone dated *The Comedy of Errors* by the lines,

Ant. S. In what part of her body stands Ireland?....
Where France?
Drom. S. In her forehead, armed and reverted, making war against her heir.

He observed,

I have no doubt that an equivoque was here intended, and that, beside the obvious sense, an allusion was intended to King Henry IV, the heir of France, concerning whose succession to the throne there was a civil war in that country, from August 1589, when his father was assassinated, for several years.

[1] Acted at the Rose, January 1594; entered Stationers' Register, February 1594.
[2] Bad Quarto entered Stationers' Register, March 1594.
[3] Bad Quarto published 1595.   [4] See page 189.
[5] Acted at Newington Butts, June 1594.
[6] Greene's *Groatsworth of Wit*.
[7] Nashe's *Pierce Penilesse* (S.R. 8 August 1592).
[8] Nashe's Preface to Greene's *Menaphon* (S.R. August 1589).

Malone's reckoning has been accepted as correct and the passage regarded as proof that at least this portion of the text cannot have been written earlier than 1589 or later than 1593, since the reference is to the civil war between Henry IV and the League; but while this reference to contemporary events is one of the few about which there need be no dubiety, Malone's historical arithmetic has been accepted unchecked. As Dr Smart[1] has pointed out Henry IV became *heir* to the French throne in 1584 on the death of the Duke of Anjou, who alone stood between him and the King; the Catholic League took up arms in 1585 to secure his exclusion; Henry won a notable victory over them in 1587, and when Henry III died in 1589 he was *king* by due inheritance and was recognized as *king* by England and other Protestant countries although the League still opposed him. He was *heir* therefore between 1584 and 1589.

It is within exactly the same period, 1584–9, that Jonson's reference in *Bartholomew Fair* (1614) fixes *Titus Andronicus*:

Hee that will sweare *Ieronimo*, or *Andronicus* are the best playes, yet, shall passe unexcepted at, heere, as a man whose Iudgement shewes it is constant, and hath stood still, these fiue and twentie, or thirtie years.

Jonson's reference to time is not as precise as one could have wished, but it undoubtedly strengthens the claim that *The Comedy of Errors* and *Titus Andronicus* are, as their debt to Plautus and Seneca suggests, among the earliest ventures of the school-

[1] *Shakespeare: Truth and Tradition*, by John S. Smart, p. 205.

master who came from Warwickshire, possibly in
1586.

It has been argued that the absence of Shakespeare's name from the Quarto editions of *Titus
Andronicus*, issued in 1594, 1600, and 1611, is a
serious objection to ascribing the play to Shakespeare.
But the three editions of *Tamburlaine* 1590, 1592,
and 1605, make no mention of Marlowe; and if it
is suggested that *Tamburlaine* proclaims its author on
every page, it must be noted that to some ears at least
this was not always clear and unmistakable. Steevens
has preserved the following note from a loose scrap
of paper in the handwriting of Dr Farmer:

Kyd—probably original author of Andronicus, Locrine,
and play in Hamlet.—Marloe of H 6.

Sporting Kyd [perhaps wrote comedy] and Marloe's
mighty line—Jonson [might assist Lily,] Perhaps Shakespeare's additions *outshone*.

Tamburlaine mentioned with praise by Heywood, as
Marloe's, might be different from the bombast one—and
that written by Kyd. (Boswell's *Malone*, XXI, 260.)

Steevens' word may be accepted on this occasion
as we know from Malone that what is not the least
ridiculous part of this note did express Farmer's considered opinion. Nor is the suspicion of some that
Farmer, however impeccable his Latin quantities,
scanned English verse with Midas' ears, a fair reply:
the lunes of Tamburlaine astonished so good an
Elizabethan as Lamb. The advance, however, in
historical knowledge of the Elizabethan drama has
swept aside Farmer's objection to ascribing the
bombast of *Tamburlaine* to Marlowe; it is permissible
to suggest that further progress may turn what is now
regarded as the decisive literary evidence for rejecting

Titus from Shakespeare's works as decisively in favour of its inclusion.

Farmer's note not only provides a reason for refusing to accept the current literary estimate of *Titus* as final, or as a sufficient makeweight to the testimony of Heminge, Condell and Meres,—for it should be noted there is no authority for ascribing *Tamburlaine* to Marlowe comparable to that which assigns *Titus* to Shakespeare—it discovers the very source of that stream of conjecture which has almost silted up the main current of Shakespearean criticism. Farmer was followed by Fleay, and Fleay by many others; they may not have the same fashion in their pretexts, conjecture is a little more ingenious, but from one we may judge them all.

Although it is not yet possible to offer any precise date for the beginning of the first period, *Titus Andronicus* and *The Comedy of Errors* can be placed at its very commencement and dated some considerable time before 1589. The period also ends in uncertainty unless it is taken as extending to the early summer of 1594 when Shakespeare, it is probable, became one of the Chamberlain's men. On their return from the provinces this Company began by acting Shakespeare's plays[1] although they had none[2] in their repertory before their departure on tour. Shakespeare himself is next heard of at Christmas as one of their three leading players;[3] his standing in the Company in 1595 strengthens the evidence that by this date he had a considerable body of successful work to his

[1] *Henslowe's Diary*, ed. Dr W. W. Greg, I, 17.

[2] *Ibid.* II, 149–57. *Henry VI* is the only one with a title that corresponds with any in the First Folio (see p. 189).

[3] *The Elizabethan Stage*, by Sir Edmund Chambers, IV, 164.

name which entitled him to his precedence. The transfer *en bloc* of his early plays to his new Company also suggests that he was already a man of sufficient means to keep control either by repurchase or agreement of his works; he was it is true a friend of Southampton by the time he joined his new Company, but his earlier work as actor and dramatist may well have enabled him to protect his interests with his own resources.

It is worth noting in passing that the end of the first period, when Shakespeare was engaged on his poems, and the Companies were on tour, may have provided the occasion for the writing of *Love's Labour's Lost*, which was written, it is generally agreed, for performance at the residence of some nobleman. *The Two Gentlemen of Verona* may also be dated before 1594, but only on internal evidence.

The place in this first period of 1, 2, 3 *Henry VI* is fixed between the date of the publication of the second edition of Holinshed's *Chronicle*, 1587,[1] and Greene's quotation from 3 *Henry VI* in 1592. It is impossible to be more precise till some future time clears up the connection between the three parts of *Henry VI* and *Richard III*, on the one hand, and *The Troublesome Reign of King John* on the other.

It was Malone who first pointed out this connection. "There are certainly", he said, "very good grounds for believing that *The Contention* and *Richard Duke of York* were written by the author or authors of the old *King John*, printed in 1591." The problem is complicated when *The Contention* and *Richard Duke of York* are reckoned among the Bad Quartos; and when some of the links between them

[1] *Shakespeare's Holinshed*, by W. G. Boswell-Stone, p. x.

and *The Troublesome Reign* are also connected with
2 and 3 *Henry VI*. If *Richard III* too is joined to it,
as it seems to be, by a few phrases further difficulties
arise. The relation of *Richard III* to another Queen's
play (*The Troublesome Reign* is assigned to that
Company on the title page), *The True Tragedie of
Richard the Third*, issued in 1594, still requires
elucidation. Two other plays assigned to the Queen's
Company, *Leir*[1] and *The Famous Victories*,[1] are also
related to work by Shakespeare. The connection
between *The Troublesome Reign*[1] and 2, 3 *Henry VI*
and *Richard III* must therefore remain for the time
undetermined, as part of a much larger problem for
which no certain solution has yet been established.

The determination of the position of *The Troublesome Reign* (1591) can hardly affect the dating of
2 and 3 *Henry VI* by more than a year, for these
latter plays must have been written by the summer of
1592, before Greene's death; this year, however, is
important as it would help to decide their relation to
Edward II. For *Richard III* the question is critical,
but must be left unanswered at this time. Such
uncertainty makes any treatment of Shakespeare's
first period work as a whole provisional, and what
follows is not offered as anything other than this.

Though the date of *Richard III* must for the
present be left undetermined, we can place 1, 2,
3 *Henry VI*, at least, in the years when Shakespeare
was writing for Lord Pembroke's Company. And

[1] Mr Dugdale Sykes and Mr Ward (*Review of English
Studies*, July 1928) have made important contributions to the
study of these plays; the present writer cannot, however, accept
the conclusions they draw from their discoveries as beyond
question.

we have some information about this Company, it is reasonable to assume, in Kyd's letter to Puckering. From it we learn that Marlowe was employed in 1591 by a noble Lord anxious to secure the work of good playwrights for his Company, but that his Lordship became alarmed at what he thought Marlowe's atheism and severed the connection. As one and one only of Marlowe's plays was produced by Pembroke's men, and as this play can be and is generally dated about 1591, it is permissible to identify the noble Lord of Kyd's letter as Pembroke. If this is correct his Company cannot have been merely, as Sir Edmund Chambers conjectures, an organization to tour the provinces; and that they played in London the title page of *Edward II* places beyond doubt; they also played at Court. Marlowe then assisted for a short period the Company to which Shakespeare belonged, and wrote for them his historical play in Shakespeare's manner.

That Marlowe had Shakespeare's *Henry VI* in mind when composing *Edward II* is maintained, it must be admitted, only on general considerations. Although Marlowe did not join Pembroke's Company till 1591 his Lordship's interest in playmakers was probably as old as 1587 when he took Kyd into his service. Whether he already had a Company by that date, or was forming one, is uncertain. By 1592 Greene can quote from 3 *Henry VI*, and if we are to believe that Shakespeare imitated Marlowe we must suppose he wrote the three parts of *Henry VI*, or at least the second and third parts, between the production of *Edward II* in 1591 and the closing of the playhouses in the summer of 1592. If *The Troublesome Reign of King John* (1591) contains echoes from

Henry VI this conclusion is impossible, and the three parts may have been written any time between 1587 and 1591. Even if they were written in the early part of that period, they may still have been designed for Pembroke's servants whose activities possibly date from 1587. We are now, however, in the midst of conjectures, but, if these are all set aside and the evidence from *John* (1591) ignored as still in dispute, general considerations from style and construction still suggest that Marlowe had the three parts of *Henry VI* in mind when composing *Edward II*.

In *Edward II* Marlowe foregoes his own high and characteristic excellence in an attempt to capture a new grace for his art. His *Tamburlaine* and *Faustus* show how he could give an individual and his desires a universal interest; it is no longer the bloodless abstraction of the Moralities with which the spectator identifies himself, for Marlowe rediscovered the protagonist of the Greeks. The Renaissance has been called the discovery of man by himself, and Marlowe's fiery energy carried the Renaissance on to the stage where he presents man and his aspirations as the chief interest of the drama. The force of this appeal is weakened in *Edward II* where he attempts a more elaborate plot, and tries to give life to more figures than his hero. When Tamburlaine is silent it is all one who speaks, Techelles or Usumcasane, one or other of the captive kings; in *Faustus* there is only the Doctor and his dreams; but in *Edward II* Marlowe tries to derive dramatic interest from the turns of the story, and to present the clash of human wills in several leading characters. This, however, is Shakespeare's particular province from the start, and from the first he is the clever contriver of the plot of intrigue: *The Comedy of Errors* and *The Taming of the Shrew* are masterpieces of construction, and, although this dexterity is not by itself so important in tragedy, it gives his *Titus Andronicus* with its torrent of horrors a smoothness not found in the dramas of Marlowe. Shakespeare's accustomed ease and certainty of design, at least, are shown in 2 and 3 *Henry VI*. In this matter *Edward II* cannot stand comparison, and beside the brilliant group of characters gathered round Henry VI, Suffolk and the Queen, Humphrey and York, Salisbury and Warwick, Clifford and Richard, the figures of Isabella and the Mortimers, Gaveston, Spenser and the rest, are no more than shadows of shades. It is permissible therefore to suppose that Marlowe was trying to improve his plotting and characterization by emulating in his *Edward II* the great craftsman with whom he had become associated. Shakespeare had no need to learn from Marlowe that skill in which 2 and 3 *Henry VI* go beyond any of Marlowe's plays; it was his from the start, so that if there is imitation in this particular it is not on Shakespeare's part.

There is no evidence that Marlowe wrote any more for Pembroke's Company than a single play, and Kyd's letter explains why this is what might be expected. Shakespeare, as the title pages of *Titus*, *a Shrew*, and *Richard Duke of York* seem to show, was more deeply engaged in their activities; but he cannot have remained a member of the Company long after Marlowe's withdrawal. A few months later the Companies were on tour, and Shakespeare could hardly have found time to write his two poems if he had also had to act in various provincial centres, and make the journey with his Company from place to place on foot or on horse; and as the poems are dedicated to a new patron, Lord Southampton, it is natural to assume that he severed his connection with Pembroke at least in 1592. Of the circumstances attending this break we know nothing, and the episode might be passed by quickly were it not a common habit with those who write about Shakespeare to present his acts in the light least favourable to his character as a man. Even Mr Crompton Rhodes in his study of Shakespeare's First Company refers to Shakespeare as the "poet of *Venus and Adonis* and *Lucrece* who had found a noble patron in the Earl of Southampton during the darkest hour of his fellows, the Earl of Pembroke's Servants".[1]

The suggestion is possible then that Shakespeare did not stand by his Company as a man might have done, or possess that sense of fellowship which is so honourable a part of the genius of Molière. Mr Crompton Rhodes may not have intended to suggest this, but there are others who do not hesitate to describe Shakespeare's actions at this time in terms which are only applicable to those whose guiding motives are purely mercenary. Writing of Shakespeare's friendship with Southampton, Professor Quincy Adams[2] says, "We may suspect that in choosing so young, extravagant, and ambitious a patron Shakespeare was exercising the shrewdness that characterised all his business enterprises"; and he quotes the letter prefixed to *Venus and Adonis* as

[1] *Shakespeare's First Folio*, by R. Crompton Rhodes, p. 91.
[2] *A Life of Shakespeare*, by Joseph Quincy Adams, p. 151. It is only fair to add that Professor Quincy Adams has removed from his account of Shakespeare's life many of the baseless suspicions with which some of his predecessors have darkened their story.

a glimpse of his "elusive personality". Those who
regard the poems as a business enterprise may well
find something "elusive" in the personality of the
man who penned for it such advertisements as the
letters to Lord Southampton.

The idea that Shakespeare was first a man of
business and then a poet goes back at least to Pope;
but his view, for which according to Sir Sidney Lee
there was just warrant, that Shakespeare

> For gain not glory winged his roving flight,
> And grew immortal in his own despite,

is a clearer record of his own frailty than a just view
of Shakespeare's genius. Pope's great poetical enterprise was an attempt to gain his financial independence
by translating Homer. It was an honourable task,
and although perhaps it strained the finer imaginative
fibre of his genius his effort commands respect for the
man as well as the poet; his conception of Shakespeare, however, was part of the price he had to pay
for the urgency in his own mind of financial gain.
Later Halliwell-Phillipps in his *Life of Shakespeare*
was to carry the idea of the great poet "working
under the domination of a Commercial spirit" across
the verge of inanity. He presents Shakespeare as a
man destitute of a cherished literary design, writing
at first only for a living and when successful for
affluence, and proceeds to gabble monstrously—the
only adequate words are Johnson's—about art.[1]

The picture has been redrawn for us in our
own time by Mr J. M. Robertson who talks of
Shakespeare's "thoroughly practical or commercial

[1] *Outlines of the Life of Shakespeare*, by J. Halliwell-
Phillipps, p. 102.

handling of the problem of life, in a calling not
usually adopted by commercially minded men".[1] He
finds the author of *Venus and Adonis*,

not much cultured, not profound, not deeply passionate;
not particularly reflective though copious in utterance; a
personality which of itself, if under no pressure of pecu-
niary need, would not be likely to give the world any
serious sign of mental capacity whatever.[2]

If copiousness of utterance and financial pressure
were the chief ingredients in genius many writers
and journalists would long ago have out-distanced
Shakespeare. And this judgment of Mr Robertson's
is strangely opposite to the opinion entertained by
Shakespeare of himself. It is clear from the Latin
motto to *Venus and Adonis* that Shakespeare then in
his thirtieth year thought of himself as a poet in the true
and direct line of inspiration; and we can hardly think
Shakespeare's judgment even in this matter inferior
to Mr Robertson's. It is true he speaks diffidently of
his own powers in the dedicatory epistle, but it would
not be natural for him when in the cool element of
prose to divulge unusual things of himself; we know
that with his singing robes about him he could speak
of his powerful verse without apology. And if we
regard *Venus and Adonis* as "consciously constructed
for the market", or a business enterprise, what are
we to make of the two preliminary letters? These
too must show that commercial shrewdness which
biographers now seem to recognize as so prominent
a trait in the poet's character, and exhibit his
"thoroughly practical or commercial handling of the
problem of life". If this is so Shakespeare was not

[1] *Shakespeare and Montaigne* (2nd ed.), p. 147.
[2] *Ibid.*

only a man of business first and a poet afterwards, he was a hypocrite and rascal before he was a man of business.

The letters themselves, however, seem to agree more with the high estimate which Shakespeare's contemporaries formed of his character, and with what we might expect from the great poet, than with the view that he was playing a dishonourable part. Those who think of Shakespeare as among the very greatest of the poets of the world, and who think of a poet as a man "endowed with more lively sensibility, more enthusiasm and tenderness, who has a greater knowledge of human nature and a more comprehensive soul" than is common among mankind, read his letters innocent of the suspicions of some of his biographers; and this or something like it is the impression they receive. The first letter is throughout modest, yet dignified and independent in its attention to the ceremonies required by the customs of the time—the barriers between one order of society and another whose proper observance the great mind, according to Dr Johnson, will not neglect. Before Shakespeare wrote again he had been disarmed by Southampton, who must have continued to receive him without condescension and probably with impetuous generosity: a mere gift however large could not have effected the change in Shakespeare's address revealed in the second letter. Without the assurance of the Earl's warm friendship Shakespeare would never have removed the cloak of his reserve, and written in the letter to his *Lucrece*, "The loue I dedicate to your Lordship is without end".

Nor is this view of Shakespeare's part in his friendship with Southampton merely the uncritical judgment of those who desire to glorify a poet in spite of truth. Tradition has recorded Southampton's bounty to Shakespeare; Rowe, who would gladly have encountered so munificent a patron, readily accepted the story; but whether we believe it or not, for Rowe was not critical in his attitude to tradition, we must remember that Southampton was as fortunate in the encounter as Shakespeare. We can still read in the poet's letter the generosity of a grateful mind at once indebted and discharged. It may be possible to be deaf to the inspiration of Shakespeare's poems and still retain some faith in one's understanding of the plays, but those who regard the two letters as other than the courteous and generous expression of the open and free nature of the creator of *Hamlet*, and the friend of Ben Jonson, cannot believe for a moment in the man we are told of by his contemporaries. If Mr Robertson's study of Shakespeare has revealed something to his critical intelligence hidden from readers who are ready to accept the poet as a great-hearted man, he has discovered what was also concealed from those who knew him most familiarly in life. "He was indeed honest", is Ben Jonson's testimony; and Jonson, who was no complaisant eulogist, set a high value on what he meant by honesty. "Of all styles", Drummond says of him, "he loved most to be named honest", and he goes on to tell how this resolute man preserved those letters in which his friends had so named him. Jonson has given Shakespeare the addition he most coveted for himself, and in this judgment he was not singular. Against the emphatic voice of Shakespeare's time present doubts about his character are worse than futile.

To suppose that he was dishonest in his dealings with his old Company is merely another uncritical conjecture. The little evidence relevant for judging Shakespeare's conduct in this particular incident apart from his general honesty is not against him. Pembroke dismissed Marlowe, and abandoned Kyd in his direst need; imprisonment and torture were unjustly inflicted on Pembroke's retainer without his Lordship's raising his voice on his behalf. It may have been more honourable to leave the Company than remain in his service.

A guess is perhaps permissible at this point in a matter on which nothing depends, but which, could we know the truth about it, might throw some light on the relation between Marlowe and Shakespeare. If we ask who it was that gave *Edward II* to the press, we may answer that it was Shakespeare, to help to keep alive the memory of the dead shepherd, once his colleague in Pembroke's Company. Marlowe's other unpublished plays in the possession of a different Company found no such guardian, and were given to the world in deplorable texts.

When Heminge and Condell came to do a similar pious office for Shakespeare's own plays they had in their possession theatrical material from these early days. Though never themselves among Pembroke's men they were able to print 2 and 3 *Henry VI* from almost flawless prompt copies once owned by that Company, as is proved by a few actors' names preserved by chance in the stage directions;[1] they were also able to restore a scene to *Titus Andronicus*

[1] *A Chronicle History of the Life and Work of William Shakespeare*, by F. G. Fleay, pp. 267–8. *Shakespeare's First Folio*, by R. Crompton Rhodes, p. 89.

although that play had been in print for thirty years. There are gaps here and there in the printed text: part of the Sly business in *The Taming of the Shrew* is missing, and *Richard III*, which they had printed from a corrected copy of the sixth Quarto, is at Act III, sc. i, ll. 17–165, and from Act v, sc. iii, l. 50 to the end, from the third Quarto.[1] These irregularities, however, may be due to some inadvertence during printing, not to the loss of early manuscript material. But when every account is made of the imperfections discovered in the Folio, the papers which contained the early work must be allowed to have been on the whole in good preservation.

There can be no doubt about Heminge and Condell being in possession of Shakespeare's papers; they tell us they made use of them, and as they had acted as the managers of the Company for many years they must have had them from Shakespeare's own hands. In 1623 they were the last survivors of the sharers who formed the Company Shakespeare joined in 1594; the shares in the Globe, amounting to half the capital outlay, which had been distributed among the actors who assisted the Burbages to finance that venture in 1598, had accumulated in their hands as their fellows dropped out one by one[2]; for the same cause what rights the actors had possessed in Shakespeare's plays would now be theirs alone. Fortunately they recognized their duty to their friend, and they claim to have taken "care and paine" in discharging it, and by the height of their care to have endeavoured to make the volume acceptable to his

[1] *A Chronicle History*, by Fleay, p. 277.
[2] *The Organization and Personnel of the Shakespearean Company*, by T. W. Baldwin, p. 111.

admirers. Twenty-four years later, when Humphrey Mosely was issuing the first folio edition[1] of Beaumont and Fletcher's plays, he uses the phrase *Care & Pains* in describing his negotiations with the owners of the manuscripts; but Heminge and Condell had no difficulty of this kind, and, if there were arrangements to be made with the publishers of the Quartos, Blount was surely the member of the partnership to see to this. It is hard to guess what duty requiring care and pain remained for Heminge and Condell but the preparation of the copy for Jaggard. The modern bibliographer and palaeographer may indeed envy Shakespeare's friends the office of collecting and publishing his writings; he could understand, however, their references to their pains if they were the correctors of the sixth Quarto of *Richard III* from which Jaggard worked: a modern editor could have prepared the copy more skilfully but hardly more laboriously.

Against this view of what Heminge and Condell mean by their care and pain, scholars can point to what now seem the wanton omissions and palpable blunders by the Folio editors; for these they blame at times some careless hireling to whom they think Heminge and Condell must have left this labour. Pope censured the first editors for using nothing better than prompt books; we are perhaps too ready to blame the corrector, who sometimes substituted for the text of the Quartos that before him in the play-

---

[1] This folio is sometimes compared with the First Folio, and arguments drawn from Mosely's shortcomings transferred to the work of Heminge and Condell. But Shakespeare's editors were not like Mosely speculative publishers, but the author's friends, admirers, and literary executors.

house manuscripts of about 1623. Heminge and
Condell would indeed have been long before their
time had they formulated for their own guidance any
satisfactory or consistent canons for dealing with
changes in Shakespeare's text. Mr Crompton
Rhodes's recent edition of Sheridan suggests some of
the difficulties they may have had to overcome. The
analysis of the differences between Folio and Quarto
texts has not yet been taken far enough to entitle us to
substitute a hired corrector for Heminge and Condell.

The editorial labours of the first editors had come
at a period in their lives when they may, as Malone
suggests, have been less closely tied to their profession
than before; Heminge was nearly seventy, and
Condell was also in his last years; they may therefore
have had some leisure to give to the task, although
less no doubt than they could have wished. We have
their own statement of the trouble they had taken;
and the scrutiny of their text by generations of
scholars has revealed the labour that must have been
expended on it. To deprive them of their full share
in this labour, even to exonerate them from its faults,
is to follow too readily perhaps, though at a distance,
the tradition of their negligence invented by their
successors in the early eighteenth century.

Of all the subsequent editors Malone was no doubt
the most entitled to question the authority of the first.
He himself had spared no pains; but his criticism of
Henry VI shows how far the safest scholar may go
astray when he rejects the guidance of Shakespeare's
friends and associates. The dissertation on these plays
is infected throughout by hasty observation, imperfect
reasoning, and ill-established conclusions. Fleay is
much more ingenious perhaps but equally mistaken;

yet he was so satisfied with his treatment of these plays that he wished this unhappy performance to be taken as a sample of the quality of his critical work as a whole. This is at once a warning and an encouragement: a warning to those who are ready to ignore on any pretext the statement that the First Folio contains Mr William Shakespeare's Comedies, Histories, and Tragedies; an encouragement to those who believe that the patient study of the text will reveal to us the nature of the True Originall Copies Heminge and Condell had in their possession. How far this faith has advanced since Professor Pollard removed the last obstacle to its progress can be seen in Mr Harley Granville-Barker's recent *Prefaces to Shakespeare*. In this imaginative and most practical interpretation of the plays he has in places to emphasize the importance for the modern producer of the text supplied by the managers of Shakespeare's own Company. The Quartos are no longer referred to as the work of pirates and the Folio as a fraudulent reprint; instead we hear of different prompt books, of the possibility that Shakespeare altered passages during production, of the claims of the Folio version. The wheel has very nearly come full circle, and the reputation of Heminge and Condell is restored to them again. Those who now set up to know better than the first editors which plays were Shakespeare's and which were not have a harder task than even Malone suspected; and one does not need to be a prophet to see that they are not likely to fare any better than that devoted scholar in their criticism of "a payre so carefull to shew their gratitude both to the liuing, and the dead", as John Heminge and Henry Condell.

INDEX

Abridged texts, 4, 165 *sq*.

Act- and scene-division, in 1 *Henry VI*, 184 *sq*.; in First Folio and Quartos, 186; in *Tamburlaine* and *Edward II*, 187 *sq*.

Actors' names substituted for characters, 17 *note*; in 2 and 3 *Henry VI*, 211

Adams, J. Quincy, explains origin of deer-stealing story, 127; on Shakespeare's business enterprise and choice of patron, 206

Additions and interpolations as evidence of revision or collaboration, 25, 185

Ajax of Sophocles quoted in *Titus Andronicus*, 140

Alcazar, performed by Strange's men, 16; Dr Greg's verdict on text applied to Quarto of *Richard III*, 166

Alleyne, Edward, acted for time with Strange's men, 15

Anticipations and *Recollections* as evidence of reporting by actors, 91 *sqq*.

Arden of Feversham, parallels with, in *Edward II*, 148; ascribed to Kyd, *ibid*.

Aubrey, John, records best authenticated tradition about Shakespeare, 7, 129 *sq*.; Beeston's statement quoted, 129; records Stratford gossip, 130; Malone's estimate of his accuracy, 131

Baconians, credulity of, 34

Bad Quartos, mainly the work of actors, 4 *sq*.; importance of plague years for their history, 4 *sq*., 71 *sq*.; contribution to study of, by Professor Pollard and Professor Dover Wilson, 3 *sq*.; by Dr Greg, 4, 65, 68 *note*, 91, 93 *note*; by Mr Rhodes, 5, 53 *sq*., 68 *sqq*.

Bartholomew Fair, reference to *Titus Andronicus* in, 198

Beeston, William, informed Aubrey that Shakespeare had been a schoolmaster, 129; confirmation of his statement in Shakespeare's early plays, 139 *sqq*.

Bernard, John, how he put together a version of *The School for Scandal*, 70 *sq*.

Blount, Edward, chief business partner in First Folio venture,

INDEX

Never too Late, criticism of the actor in, 43 *sq.*

Observer, The, quoted on authorship of *Richard II*, 33
"Old" plays, Malone's protest against multiplication of, 175
Old Wives Tale, 18
Orlando, 16, 17 *note*, 68 *note*
Ovid, influence on Shakespeare, 141, admired by Elizabethans, *ibid.*

Peele, connection with Queen's Company, 18; Mr Dugdale Sykes attributes *Leir* and *The Troublesome Reign* to, 20; Joan of Arc libels in 1 *Henry VI* pair with his on Queen Elinor in *Edward II*, 24; possible share in *Henry VI* and *Richard III*, 24 *sq.*; addressed by Greene, 41; possible share in *Edward II*, 147
Pembroke, Henry Herbert, second earl of, relations with Kyd and Marlowe, 202 *sq.*, 211; his Company, 12, 21, 203
Pembroke, William Herbert, third earl of, friendly to Burbage, 36
Pembroke's Company, doubts as to their existence before 1592, 12; Sir Edmund Chambers' theory of their origin, 21; failure in 1593, 71 *sq.*; possessed Shakespeare's early plays, 10 *note*, 30, 72, 191, 202, 211; and Marlowe's *Edward II*, 94, 203 *sq.*
Pericles, excluded from Folio, 23, 122, 143; thought by Farmer Shakespeare's first venture, 122
Pickwick, Bardell *v.*, cited for use of *his* before quotation, 48
Plague of 1592–3, place in Shakespeare's career of, 196
Plautus, in Elizabethan schools, 8; Shakespeare's borrowings from, 139 *sq.*
Pollard, A. W., provides foundation for criticism of Shakespeare text and canon by (i) his estimate of copy used for Good Quartos and First Folio, 37; (ii) his interpretation of phrase "stolne and surreptitious" which vindicates good faith of first editors, 37, 134 *sq.*, 215; on Malone's theory about 2 and 3 *Henry VI*, 2 *sq.*, 22; on Bad Quartos, 3 *sqq.*; on Malone's misinterpretation of Greene's attack on Shakespeare, 6; estimate of Aubrey's evidence, 7; on Shakespeare's small Latin, 8; on Shakespeare's early plays, 8 *sqq.*; on Shakespeare's first Company, 11 *sqq.*; on possibility of collaboration in Folio plays, 23; probability of theories proposed considered, 23 *sqq.*; interpretation of bibliographical

estimate of his powers in motto and dedicatory epistle to, 195, 208; Mr Robertson's appreciation of, 208

Verse tests, the rhyme test, 26 *sqq.*; double endings, 104 *sq.*, 150 *sq.*; still crude and undeveloped, 152

Warburton, on *Henry VI*, 39

Warwick, actor playing, his report of York's pedigree, 56–58; share in closing scenes of 2 *Henry VI*, 75; his part in Quartos compared with that of others, *ibid.*; collaborates with colleague, 75, 82, 89; difference his presence makes to quality of report, 113

Whole Contention, The, corrections in, without manuscript authority, 106–110

Wilkinson, Tate, constructs version of *The Duenna*, 69

Wilson, J. Dover, study of Bad Quartos with Professor Pollard, 3 *sq.*; finds "old" plays behind *The Comedy of Errors* and *The Taming of the Shrew*, 8; evidence that *A Midsummer Night's Dream* was revised by Shakespeare, 26; on Jaggard's corrections in 1619 volume, 110; his application of Professor Pollard's conclusions to text, 135; on *Taming of a Shrew*, 142 *note*

Winter's Tale, ascription to Shakespeare questioned by Pope, 36

Wise, Andrew, published *Richard III*, 30

York's pedigree, in *The Contention* and 2 *Henry VI*, 60 *sqq.*; in *The Whole Contention*, 106 *sq.*